WARRIOR
SECRETS

Keith Yates

WARRIOR SECRETS

A HANDBOOK OF THE MARTIAL ARTS

KEITH YATES
6TH DAN

FOREWORD
BY
RAYMOND
McCALLUM

Paladin Press
Boulder, Colorado

Warrior Secrets
A Handbook of the Martial Arts
by Keith Yates
Copyright © 1985 by Keith Yates

ISBN 0-87364-306-2
Printed in the United States of America

Published by Paladin Press, a division of
Paladin Enterprises, Inc., P.O. Box 1307,
Boulder, Colorado 80306, USA.
(303) 443-7250

Direct inquiries and/or orders to the above address.

ACKNOWLEDGMENTS

Thanks to my many friends in the
martial arts who helped me
in compiling this book.

Photographers include David Edmonson, Arnold Howard,
Joe Duke, and Keith Yates.
Cover and inside illustrations by Keith Yates.

*Dedicated to my three future black belts,
Ryan, Randall, and Regan.*

THE AUTHOR

Keith D. Yates is a sixth degree black belt in Korean
tae kwon-do. He is a veteran of twenty years of martial arts
practice earning additional black belts in ju-jutsu and kobudo. Mr. Yates is a former kata champion and is recognized
as a forms expert. He has written numerous articles for
martial arts publications and contributed to textbooks on
physical education and karate weapons. This is his second
book, the first being *The Complete Book of Taekwon Do
Forms* (Paladin Press). Mr. Yates did his master's thesis on
the martial arts power of "ki." He is the founder and president of the Southwest Taekwon-Do Association.

Foreword

As I travel around the world, I am amazed at how the martial arts have skyrocketed in popularity in the last few years. While I am excited to see this, I am also disturbed at the confusion this rapid growth has generated, with new schools and new styles being created—almost daily. Although we can't stop the charlatans from operating, we can educate the public in the *real essence* of the martial arts.

When I started karate in 1972, Keith D. Yates was one of the black belt instructors I had the pleasure of working out with. His many years in the martial arts make him an ideal person to compile a book like *Warrior Secrets*. Although there are other so-called handbooks on the martial arts, most of them only contain the views and opinions of one man, the author. What makes Keith's book different, I think, is the interviews he has included with so many experts. This way, the reader can be assured of getting a variety of perspectives on each art and can come to his or her own conclusions.

I'm proud to have been able to play a small part in this volume, and I'm sure you'll appreciate and enjoy it as much as I have.

RAYMOND McCALLUM

U.S. Karate Champion and former
World Full-Contact Champion

Contents

Introduction

Fifteen years ago, if you asked the average person what kung fu was, he would probably have answered "an appetizer at Chung King's Chinese take out." But today karate, judo, and kung fu are commonly known. In just barely over ten years the number of martial arts schools in the United States has tripled. There are one-and-a-half million Americans practicing the Korean art of tae kwon-do alone.

What has caused this dramatic growth in interest in the warrior arts? Perhaps it is the search for religious enlightenment that some Westerners think they might glean from these Oriental disciplines. Maybe it's due to the media fascination with shows like TV's "Kung Fu" and the cinema's Bruce Lee and Chuck Norris. Probably crime statistics have something to do with it. The last decade has shattered all records for stranger-to-stranger crime, with violent assaults up over 60 percent nationwide.

Whatever the reasons, the martial arts craze continues to skyrocket, with Americans flocking to various schools and studios for a taste of the "martial mystique." Unfortunately, most people still don't know the difference between karate and tae kwon-do, judo and ju-jutsu, aikido and tai chi, and so on. Since there are no nationwide standards for these arts, it is pretty easy for a green or blue belt in one city to move up the road to the next town and set up shop proclaiming himself tenth degree black belt and "former World Champion."

In this book I'm going to give you an education in the most popular martial arts in America. We'll explore the traditions of each art and its historical development. We'll look at both the physical and the mental aspects of training, and we'll hear from some of the most well-known proponents of these modern warrior disciplines to get their views and secrets. Also included are photos of self-defense techniques against common street attacks. By comparing the approach of each system, you will be able to see where they are similar and where they are different.

If you're already a martial artist, I think you'll find out some things you've never known before, and if you have never studied any art, I hope you'll get out your Yellow Pages after you've finished reading this book and look up the nearest school. By then you should know what to look for and what questions to ask so that you can be assured of getting quality instruction.

CHAPTER ONE

The Historical Aspects

Tracing The Warrior Tradition

Almost all cultures have a fighting tradition. Hieroglyphics from 4000 B.C. found in the ancient sands of Egypt portray an unarmed combat similar to boxing. Homer described the Greek methods of fighting in his *Iliad*. The apostle Paul used analogies of combat in his New Testament teaching.

The highest levels of martial arts, however, have been developed in the Far East; in fact, the very term *martial arts* has come to signify, in most people's minds, the Oriental fighting disciplines. Historical background information for these combative arts is obscure and clouded with fantasy and folklore. Combine that with the fact that the classifications of karate and kung fu alone represent hundreds, perhaps thousands, of various styles, and you can see how no one can keep up with all of it.

Still, I think the best place to start our study is with a look into the backgrounds of the martial arts. Hopefully you will not only begin to get a better feel for the traditional aspects of these time-honored arts but will also gain a new respect for them.

While historians differ on many of the details, most trace the earliest forms of systematized fighting to ancient India and China.

India

There was a time in India's history when warfare was common, with many different factions vying with each other for supremacy. It was during these pre-Christian times that a warrior class known as the *kshatriya* arose. Although it is next to impossible to document the details of any formal type of ancient fighting art in India due to conflicting and often ambiguous texts, we do know from certain sources that there appeared to be an emphasis on the clenched fist (known as *vijra-mushti*) and perhaps even prearranged exercises, like modern karate's forms.

Fig. 1 This drawing is based on a typically wild- and ferocious-looking portrait of *Bodhidharma* painted in the sixteenth century. It was ten decades before that, in the sixth century, that the Indian monk Bodhidharma (Daruma in Japanese) is said to have journeyed to the Chinese Shaolin monastery. To help the monks withstand the long hours of meditation that he demanded he taught a series of physical exercises. From his meditative approach to Buddhism sprang the Ch'an sect of Buddhism (Zen in Japan) and from his exercises, it is said, comes Shaolin Temple boxing. There is little written on this mysterious and legendary monk and some doubt that he ever really existed. Yet to many he retains a place of honor as the patron saint of the warrior arts.

Today, the art of *kalaripayit,* which utilizes both empty-hand and weapons techniques, is practiced mainly in southwest India. There are other Indian fighting arts as well, but they are practically unheard of outside of the subcontinent.

China

The man acknowledged by many as the father of the karatelike arts was an Indian Buddhist monk known as Bodhidharma (Ta-mo in Chinese and Daruma in Japanese), who was a member of the warrior class in India as a young man. From his teachings sprang the *dhyana,* or meditative school of Buddhism called *Ch'an* by the Chinese and better known in the West by its Japanese name, *Zen.* Bodhidharma traveled to China around 520 A.D. in order to spread his teachings of meditation and Buddhism. This Zen patriarch ended up residing at the Shaolin-ssu Monastery in Hohon Province.

There at the Shaolin Temple, he devised and began to teach the monks a system of integrated physical, mental, and spiritual discipline similar to yoga exercises. His original eighteen moves were probably influenced by his training and earlier experiences in India. As the years passed, his exercises were further developed and became known as *Shaolin ch'uan fa,* which can be defined as "the way of combat" (although it has several dialectical interpretations). For centuries it was practiced by the monks in secrecy.

It is said that Bodhidharma never intended his system to become a method of combat, for his purposes and teachings were aimed at cultivating the minds and spirits of his followers through peaceful meditation. Legend says that at one point during a long meditation period he unwittingly fell asleep. To prevent it from happening again, he cut off his own eyelids right then and there.

Regardless of Bodhidharma's intentions, however, his system was later used by the monks to defend themselves against marauding bands of outlaws who roamed the country-side. It was also taught to neighboring farmers for their own self-protection.

Today there are literally hundreds of styles in the Shaolin kung fu family that trace their roots back to Bodhidharma and even earlier, for we know that there were fighting disciplines in China even before the sixth century. Chinese martial arts are frequently split into external hard systems on one hand and internal soft systems on the other. In a way this is misleading because it suggests a rigid division of the two. To the Chinese everything contains, at least in part, its opposite (the concept of Yin and Yang). All external hard styles therefore contain some softer techniques, and hard techniques can even be found in the softest style of all, *tai chi chuan.* In general terms, however, we can say that the external styles *(wei chia)* emphasize speed and power with strong stable stances while internal styles *(nei chia)* stress the health benefits of their art with more emphasis on control and internal energy, or *ch'i.*

Kung fu can further be divided into northern and southern styles. Because north China has mostly grasslands, long steps and sweeping kicks were effective. The south was more urbanized with many people living on boats. Footwork was therefore not as active, and more emphasis was placed on rapid hand movements, utilizing the southerners' strong oarsmen's torsos.

Southeast Asia

As Buddhism spread into neighboring Southeast Asian kingdoms, Shaolin ch'uan fa spread with it. Wherever it went, it became integrated with the indigenous martial and spiritual traditions of that locale to form new and unique entities. Cambodia, Vietnam, and Indonesia all developed systems of combat. Perhaps the best known art from this area is Thai kick boxing *(muay thai),* which is very similar to today's

CHINA

INDIA

VIETN

Fig. 2 The martial arts of the Far East
and their countries of origin.

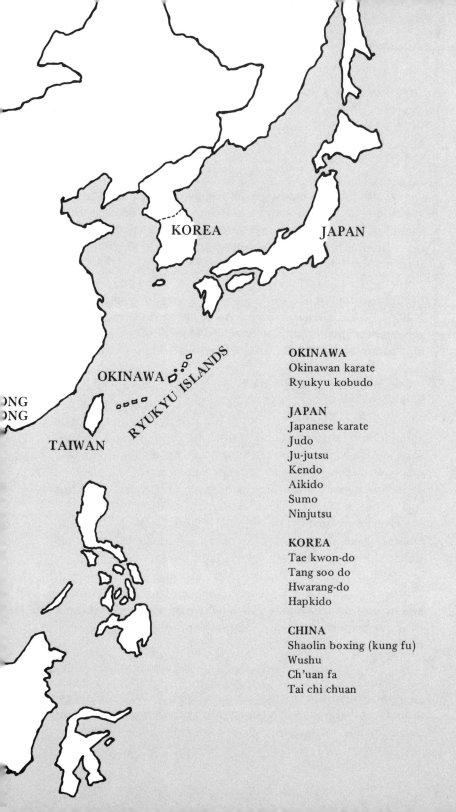

KOREA

JAPAN

OKINAWA
Okinawan karate
Ryukyu kobudo

JAPAN
Japanese karate
Judo
Ju-jutsu
Kendo
Aikido
Sumo
Ninjutsu

KOREA
Tae kwon-do
Tang soo do
Hwarang-do
Hapkido

CHINA
Shaolin boxing (kung fu)
Wushu
Ch'uan fa
Tai chi chuan

OKINAWA

RYUKYU ISLANDS

ONG
ONG

TAIWAN

full-contact karate, only with fewer rules and less padding. More than a few deaths have resulted from this violent sport.

Okinawa

Of the many countries that have contributed to the evolution of the modern martial arts tradition, the little island of Okinawa is one of the most important. While it must be pointed out, again, that much of the history of the warrior arts has been pieced together from many different sources, it seems apparent that ch'uan fa techniques were brought from China to Okinawa (the main island of the Ryukyu Islands) before 1000 A.D. These skills, along with other local techniques, slowly developed into a uniquely Okinawan system of purely hand techniques known as *tode* or "Chinese hands."

Early in the seventeenth century Japan overran Okinawa and placed severe restrictions on daily activities. Because the islanders were denied weapons, the various factions of tode and ch'uan fa practitioners united to combat their oppressors, and a system known simply as *te,* meaning "hand," emerged. Since these early groups were forced underground to escape detection by the Japanese samurai, most of our history of this movement is based on oral tradition.

Over the centuries three major Okinawan styles began to emerge, each named after the areas where they were practiced. They were *shuri-te, naha-te,* and *tomari-te.* Today there are several styles of Okinawan karate including *isshin-ryu, shorin-ryu,* and *goju-ryu.* There is also an Okinawan weapons system known as *ryuku-kobudo* which specializes in the use of farm implements forged into weapons such as the *nunchaku, tonfa,* and *sai.*

Japan

Like other Eastern kingdoms, Japan had forms of unarmed combat very early in its history. There is an ancient tale (23 B.C.) of the emperor ordering a man named Nomi-no-Sukune to battle with the most fierce and merciless wrestler of the day. Nomi-no-Sukune proceeded to kick and punch the wrestler to death. Perhaps he was one of the early fathers of *bujutsu*, the Japanese martial arts.

The ancient bujutsu were steeped in Shinto and Buddhist dogma and the beginnings of the early *ryu* or various styles are cloaked with mysticism. The Japanese *bushi* (also known as samurai) developed styles around every weapon of the day, from *ken-jutsu* (sword), to *kyu-jutsu* (bow and arrow), to *ba-jutsu* (horsemanship). At about the beginning of the seventh century came the first cultural exchange between Japan and China and, no doubt, some forms of ch'uan fa were introduced as well, for there are certain similarities between *ju-jutsu*, one of Japan's oldest unarmed arts, and the Shaolin methods.

Warring ceased to be a dominant feature of Japanese life with the founding of the Tokugawa Shogunate in 1603. The bushi's need for battlefield skills was reduced, so these warriors began to develop nonmartial activities such as the tea ceremony and even flower arranging. From this movement came a new approach to the martial arts based largely on the Chinese concept of the *Tao* or "way," which came to be known as *budo* or "martial ways." Taking form between the seventeenth and nineteenth centuries, the "classical" budo became more spiritual in their goals, aiming toward a kind of self-realization through physical training. Ken-jutsu became *kendo;* arts like *aiki-jutsu* and *ju-jutsu* gave way to the more popular arts of *aikido* and *judo*. The journey of the martial arts in Japan continues to this day; many practice them mainly for exercise and sport, although there does remain a spiritual emphasis among the more traditional masters.

In 1882, Jigoro Kano, an innovative educator and student of ju-jutsu, founded a new art which he called judo. Most of the old bujutsu systems did not include competition because it was believed that anything but actual combat is far too dangerous and that modifying the techniques for sport weakens them. Basically what Kano did was to combine the traditional disciplines with modern educational theory. Judo, which means "the way of flexibility," uses a variety of dynamic throws and powerful locks and pins specifically designed for competition. Judo's popularity is great; it has, in fact, become an Olympic sport, the first martial art to be so recognized (tae kwon-do has been approved for inclusion in the 1988 Olympics).

Another modern Japanese martial art is aikido. Its founder, Morihei Ueshiba, in 1925 tried to develop a system in which the emphasis was on the unification of mind and body where self-defense could be accomplished without injuring the attacker. Breath control, meditation and ethical principles are all integral parts of aikido. In chapter three we will dig a little deeper into the mental and spiritual aspects of this fascinating art.

Karate itself is also a relative latecomer to the Japanese martial arts scene. Gichin Funakoshi was an Okinawa-te master and public school teacher who demonstrated his art in Japan for the first time in 1922. It met with great favor and before long was instituted into the public school curriculum under the name *karate-jutsu*. Funakoshi was the one who changed the concept of *kara*, which was originally written with an ideogram meaning China, to another ideogram, still pronounced *kara*, meaning empty. Thus karate, China-hand, 空手 became karate, empty hand 空手 .

Funakoshi soon established his own style in Japan, calling it *shotokan*. Other styles of uniquely Japanese karate soon sprang up. Hidenori Otsuka modified the Okinawan system into *wado-ryu*. Yamaguchi Goen, popularly known as "the cat," devised his *goju* style as a combination of hard and soft actions. Mas Oyama, the man credited with introducing karate into the United States, took his knowledge of Chinese and Korean arts and added elements from shotokan and goju to create *kyokushinkai.* Today there are over a hundred different schools of karate in Japan. The Japanese gave their karate a different approach than the Okinawans. Funakoshi, for example, was a traditional Okinawan master who disapproved of free-style sparring and gave *kata* (prearranged patterns) preeminence in his style. Ironically, shotokan today places heavy emphasis on competition, as do most other Japanese schools.

Korea

The origins of tae kwon-do, also called the Korean style of karate, can be traced back into ancient history. Ruins from the Koguryo dynasty, founded roughly at the time of Christ, bear figures in seemingly ancient martial arts practice.

Ch'uan fa was introduced into Korea along with Buddhism, and evolved into the ancient art of *subak.* The art at first flourished only on temple grounds, with an intricate interweaving of spiritual and physical aspects. Later the techniques were passed on to the common people, for the times were especially violent, with three kingdoms warring for control of the land.

The kingdom of Silla was finally victorious, and in 688 A.D. a unified kingdom over all Korea was established. Silla is recognized for its *Hwarang-Do,* a patriotic and philosophical movement which emphasized a high moral code along with martial arts practice. Its members were much like the Japanese samurai or English knights.

In the early tenth century Silla was overthrown by a warlord who set up the Koryo dynasty. During this period subak (also called *tae kyon* by this time) was elevated to a great popularity among the general populace. This era produced fierce warriors who many times successfully defended the kingdom against its enemies. But, inevitably, their rule declined and was replaced by the Yi dynasty, which held scholarship in higher esteem than the martial arts; as a result tae kyon practice declined.

In 1910, the Japanese overran Korea and banned the use of weapons and martial arts practice altogether. During this occupation the Korean art went into hiding. Several different names came into use, including *tang soo* and *hwa soo*. The end of World War II brought thousands of Koreans back home from China and Japan, where they had been exposed to other forms of combat. As part of a national movement to restore Korean traditions, many martial arts schools were opened under a variety of names. In 1955, the leading masters decided on a new name, suggested by Korean General Choi Hong Hi: tae kwon-do, meaning "the way of kicking and punching."

Once unified, tae kwon-do has today splintered into several rival organizations. The official Korean group, the World Tae Kwon-Do Federation, has succeeded in getting their version into the Olympic games, beginning, appropriately enough, in 1988 in Seoul, Korea.

I should also mention several other popular Korean arts. *Tang soo do* is basically a hard style similar to tae kwon-do. It enjoys a separate reputation because of several well-known practitioners, including movie star Chuck Norris. The art of the aforementioned Hwarang-Do survives today in various styles. The martial art called *hwarang-do* consists of circular techniques with many holds, throws, and takedowns. It also places much emphasis on the art of healing. *Hapkido,* which also traces its roots back to the Hwarang-Do (although it was only formally founded in 1940), has techniques that are generally not geared for competition as in tae kwon-do but are used strictly for real-life combat, reminiscent of the Japanese bujutsu attitudes.

United States

Martial arts were practically unheard of in the United

States until after World War II. No real growth came until after the Korean war when many Americans brought home judo, karate, and tae kwon-do skills after being stationed in the Far East.

A big boost to karate exposure was the American tour of the aforementioned Mas Oyama in 1952. Oyama at first demonstrated karate by showing the various training patterns of kata. But the American audiences seemed more amused than impressed until Oyama began his barehanded breaking of boards and bricks. Although breaking is a very small part of a karate education, there are still those who think that is all we do; they expect you to be able to smash through several inches of wood or concrete if you are taking lessons.

In the United States the most popular martial arts are karate, tae kwon-do, judo, aikido, and kung fu, with karate and tae kwon-do being the most prevalent, although kung fu has received much publicity and growth as of late.

In the remainder of this book we will take a closer look at these arts, especially the way they are practiced in America.

CHAPTER TWO

The Physical Aspects

A Survey

In order to give you a more complete understanding of the technical aspects of the martial arts, this chapter is devoted to an examination of the external, or physical, skills themselves. As we have already seen, there are a myriad of arts developed by many different Eastern cultures, so the variety of techniques is bound to be tremendous. Indeed, there are many technical variations, but while the theoretical bases and even purposes of each art may differ, we see a broad similarity between all systems. Because of this a basic survey is possible.

Please note that these are general divisions, and rare is the system that will be exclusively confined to any one category. My purpose in this chapter necessitates brevity; for a more detailed look at any of the arts mentioned, find a book on the subject or check out a competent instructor in your neighborhood.

Figure 3 is a chart that may help you in comparing the arts. Almost all martial arts techniques can be divided into two very broad categories which we will call *grappling* and *striking*.

Grappling

Grappling systems include gripping, wrestling, throwing, and holds, including joint-locks, chokes, and strangles. Grappling employs short-range techniques (unlike striking) and necessitates quite close physical contact. Familiar examples are judo, ju-jutsu, aikido, and wrestling.

The Grip

In most systems that involve primarily grappling techniques there is a formal gripping position. The judo posture (illustrated in fig. 4), the Graeco-Roman wrestling position, and certain aikido attack positions all prepare the two opponents for combat.

Martial Arts Comparison Chart

	AIKIDO	BOXING	JUDO	JU-JUTSU	KARATE	KUNG FU	TAE KWON-DO	WRESTLING
GRAPPLING								
Throws	●		●	●				
Takedowns	●		●	●	●	●	●	●
Holds & Locks	●		●	●				●
Strangles			●	●				
Nerve Centers & Pressure Points	●		●	●	●	●	●	
STRIKING								
Punching		●		●	●	●	●	
Open Hand Blows			●	●	●	●	●	
Kicking				●	●	●	●	
Block & Parries	●	●		●	●	●	●	

Fig. 3   Martial arts comparison chart.

Fig. 4 Vince Tamura (left) demonstrates the standard judo grip.

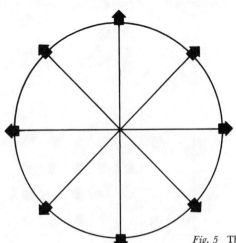

Fig. 5 The eight directions of balance taught in judo and other martial arts.

The grip can also serve as a means to control the opponent's movement. In fact, grips and grip-breaking are considered by the coaches of the U.S. Judo Association as one of the "Eight Elements of Judo Contesting." In aikido the simple gesture of a grasped wrist can be developed into a powerful technique capable of virtually controlling the opponent's offensive capabilities, something we will examine more closely in the chapter on aikido.

The Throw

The most spectacular aspect of grappling is perhaps the throw. Here you are actually using the ground as a striking surface to hit your opponent. It is advisable to always practice throws on a mat. In one of the few injuries I've incurred over my years of martial arts practice, I landed just off the edge of a mat while being thrown during a judo practice and smashed my ankle on the floor. It swelled up like a baseball, and it was a couple of weeks before I could walk without limping, let alone train at full speed.

The key factor in throwing is the center of balance. A smaller and lighter man or woman can easily throw a larger attacker if the center of balance is upset. This disruption of the opponent's balance can be accomplished in any one of eight directions (see fig. 5).

Another important factor in a throw is the analysis of the attacker's base of support. It is often thought that a direct application of force is the best way to upset the opponent's balance, but a skilled fighter will easily avoid such a push or pull. In almost all fighting arts, skill and subtlety are used rather than direct force.

Essentially, you want to get an attacker's upper body moving faster than his feet. A basic technique for doing so is to use the adversary's own momentum against him. In judo it is "pull when pushed/push when pulled," often seizing an oncoming opponent by the clothes and then throwing and pinning him or her. In aikido, an emphasis is placed on turning, much like a revolving door, when attacked. Wrestling utilizes a slightly different approach but the same basic principles. Approximately 70 percent of all takedowns in Western wrestling at the championship level have been found to be variation of leg dives, also known as leg tackles and leg pickups.

Groundwork

Techniques that work on the ground are a necessity because so many real-life fights consist of rolling around on the floor rather than a clean-cut exchange of standing punches.

I can remember first sparring with judo people. I would throw a kick to the back of a guy's head, controlling it within an inch or so, and then he would rush in and try to throw me. When I informed him that I had just "knocked him out" with a roundhouse kick he usually replied with something like, "Aw, that wouldn't have stopped me." Whether it would have or not, it got me thinking about what might happen if I couldn't get a kick off or if it was deflected and then some guy got me on the ground. That's when I decided to become familiar with some judo and ju-jutsu techniques.

Ground wrestling is highly developed in both judo and in wrestling. Judo, in particular, utilizes many joint-locks and body-weight controls. These can be shifted smoothly and changed quickly in case the first one proves to be ineffective. In wrestling, several effective techniques are considered illegal, and so a variety of highly skillful circular body shifts have been developed.

Many judo or wrestling pins, however, would not be suitable in a true combat situation where biting, pinching, clawing, and so on are not prohibited (remember that judo and wrestling are both primarily sports). In such cases, some of the throws of aikido and ju-jutsu, where a hold-down follows, would be more viable. These types of hold-down usually involve the opponent on his face with one arm or hand restrained by a painful joint-lock. It seems I would always go home much sorer from a ju-jutsu workout than I ever did from a karate class. Of course, I was in a class of karate black belts taking ju-jutsu, and I suspect that our instructor tried his best to show us how effective his art was by being especially rough on us!

Joint-locks, while versatile and effective, are generally difficult to apply against a stronger attacker because of the amount of skill needed before they can be accurately applied. Positioning, timing, and considerable practice are all vital for an effective joint-lock. There is a great temptation for an inexperienced fighter to try to force a failed attempt. If there is not an immediate flow into a different technique, you are likely to find yourself in a strength contest, something you don't want in most real-life situations.

Strangles and Chokes

These could best be termed supplementary techniques. They are an important part of ju-jutsu and judo, although illegal in wrestling competition.

The ordinary choke is described as applied pressure against the windpipe in order to cut off the person's air supply. Unconsciousness can take as long as sixty seconds to produce. If applied by a very strong grip or if the throat is hit by a hard blow, the windpipe could even be crushed. Several police departments forbid the use of a choke hold because it has resulted in fatalities.

A more widely used martial arts choke is the arterial strangle which applies pressure to the carotid arteries on either side of the neck. When both arteries (which carry the blood supply to the brain) are compressed, it takes only six seconds or so to produce a rapid loss of blood pressure and unconsciousness. As in the choke above, recovery of consciousness is usually spontaneous as long as the pressure has not been continued past the point of unconsciousness.

Incidentally, the so-called nerve strangle or death choke is nothing more than a myth, according to Dr. Gabriel Fried, a prominent Dallas physician experienced in athletic injuries. "Extreme pressure on the carotid arteries could cause a reflex stoppage of the heart in older people, but a younger man, in reasonably good shape, shouldn't suffer any permanent damage as long as you don't keep choking him after he blacks out," says Dr. Fried. "That's the only way you could kill someone with a strangle. There isn't any place on the neck where you can just drop someone with a touch, like Mr. Spock."

Striking

We will define this as the second major division of martial arts technique. It is a longer range technique than grappling,

Fig. 6 Weight plus speed equals power. If a smaller object (the Volkswagen) travels at very great speed it can generate as much power as a larger object (the Cadillac) travelling at a slower speed. Therefore a smaller person can be as powerful as a larger person by utilizing body momentum and speed.

and the taller, longer-reaching person will naturally have a slight advantage, although this can be overcome through the use of speed. I'm very limber but I'm only five-foot-eight and have always had to rely on my speed when sparring a bigger opponent, which most of them have been, unfortunately.

There is an unbelievable variety of techniques within this category and so, again, we can only go over a few of the basic types in this study. They will all utilize as weapons the hands, the feet, the knees, the elbows, and sometimes even the head.

The essence of a strike is to generate power or momentum and then to transmit it via an impact area to the opponent's body. The power of a strike is made up of two parts: weight and speed, with speed being the more important (see fig. 6). Double the weight of the attacking object and you double the power of the blow; double the speed at which it travels and the power is multiplied by four!

Hands—Punching

Anyone who has seen a John Wayne movie thinks he knows how to throw a punch. That kind of wind-up, knock-'em-through-the-window punch is, however, slow and comparatively weak.

More often than not a karate punch will travel in a straight line. The most frequently used method for generating body momentum is a rapid twisting of the hips. This can involve a rapid extension of the rear leg and a shooting forward of the body as the pelvis rotates. Boxing and karate both utilize this approach even though they apply it a little differently. A forward step preceding the punch also adds greatly to the force, although it is not always practical to step in such a manner. The rotation of the wrist is another way to add snap, and thus power, to a punch. This turning of the wrist is a standard karate maneuver.

The biggest obstacle to developing a powerful punch is

the tendency to contract the arm and shoulder muscles and
try to hit hard. This can slow down the punch considerably.
An untrained, "wind-it-up-and-throw-it" approach can
easily be seen coming and the skilled fighter can block or
even counterstrike before the punch has arrived.

A boxer or karateka therefore practices punching with no
wind-up, giveaway preparation and with a maximum focus of
power into the strike. The mental emphasis is on the attack
itself and not on the preparation for it. At the advanced
stages a fighter will focus also on the withdrawal of the fist
or the snap-back. The punch is snapped back as fast as it was
thrust out. This whiplash effect concentrates a penetrating
shock force into the target area and is extremely hard to
detect coming when properly executed. The return to the
starting position also prepares the fighter to better defend
himself with blocks or to deliver another blow.

This type of punch can only be developed through much
practice, and the building up of speed should be accomplished slowly. The arm is never to be locked at the elbow at
full extension, as it is thus subject to injury and slows the
retraction considerably.

Other hand strikes include finger thrusts, blows with the
side of the hand (chops), palm heel hits, and elbows. Training these natural body weapons is a matter of acquiring
precision and coordination. Contrary to popular belief, the
development of callouses and toughening of the skin on the
hands has little effect on the effectiveness of the blow on
such a soft surface as the human body and can be, in fact,
damaging to the proper functioning of the hand in the long
run. I can personally remember doing bounce knuckle push
ups on concrete floors.

"The human hand is not built to handle that kind of
jolt," says Dr. Fried. "I can guarantee you'll get arthritis
much sooner than you'd get it otherwise. I recommend you
use protective gloves when you spar and training gloves when

working on the heavy bag. Hand injuries—besides being painful—are extremely expensive and very difficult to fix as good as before."

Feet—Kicking

Kicks are so effective that some fighting systems use them totally in preference to punches and other hand techniques, e.g., French savate. While kicks are harder to control and the reduced base of support, with only one foot on the ground, can leave you temporarily vulnerable, the advantages of reach and power are an effective combination. This is because the leg muscles are several times stronger than the arm muscles and, of course, the leg is also longer than the arm. So by kicking you are able to land a more powerful blow while simultaneously protecting your vital points from an opponent's strikes.

Fig. 7 Karate kicks must be delivered with proper balance as shown in the middle illustration. At left the figure is leaning too far to the rear while the figure at right is leaning too far forward.

The fundamental factor to remember while kicking is balance. To remain in a balanced state during a kick, your center of gravity must fall within the base of support. If your center of gravity is too far to the rear, you can too easily be pushed off balance when your foot hits the target. If it is too far forward, you are in danger of falling forward if you miss or are deflected off target (fig. 7).

Perhaps the strongest kick is the side thrust kick. Due to the twist of the hips on delivery, much power and reach can be developed. If properly practiced, it can also be very fast. You will see two kinds of side kicks, a blade of the foot attack used most often in Japanese karate and a heel of the foot strike employed by Korean tae kwon-do (fig. 8).

An accomplished fighter will integrate both kicks and punches into combative techniques. For example, the kick can be low, drawing the opponent's guard down, and the punch can be thrown to the now open head area.

While kicks can be delivered anywhere by a limber

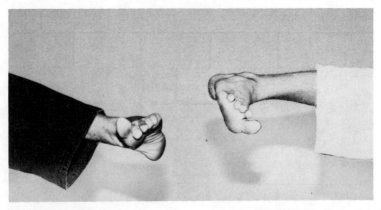

Japanese Side Kick　　　　　　　　**Korean Side Kick**

Fig. 8 The Japanese styles of karate most often employ a side kick striking with the blade of the foot. Korean systems, however, make use of the heel as a striking surface.

fighter, and while you may see some spectacular kicks in movies or on contact-karate on TV, in an actual situation low kicks (knees and groin) are *much* more effective, not to mention easier to do. They are so damaging, in fact, that they are not even allowed in competition.

Blocks

The defensive counterpoint to the strike is the block. Blocks can vary as much from style to style as the strikes themselves. Some, quite powerful, can slam against an attacker's arm or leg with enough force to break it. In other systems, a light slap diverts the attack so that it misses the intended target. An even more subtle block deflects the blow with a gentle glide of the hand to merely redirect its force.

While blocks can be used in a purely defensive manner, they are more often combined with a counterattack. This could be a throw, a joint-lock, or a punch or kick strike. A good counter must be thrown *immediately* after the block so the opponent cannot throw a second technique or withdraw into a defensive position. An even more effective method of counterattack would be launched at the exact time as the block. This simultaneous movement is obviously faster but is also much more difficult to execute properly.

Evasion

Evasion involves ducking, bobbing, and weaving to avoid strikes. You see little of it in the harder karate traditions, but it is often employed in sword and stick fighting, and Western boxing has developed it to a fine art. Withdrawing to get out of an opponent's reach and body spinning to avoid the line of attack are also found in most wrestling disciplines.

Hard vs. Soft

It is important to any study of the systems of martial arts that one be aware of the fundamental difference between what are known as "hard" and "soft" styles. In general, these two schools of thought can be defined as linear vs. circular techniques, although there naturally is some combination of the two in any system.

A typical hard system, like Korean tae kwon-do or shoto-kan karate, will emphasize direct, piercing techniques, combining strong muscular energy and intense mental concentration. The fundamental principle is that force is opposed by force. The movements will be very quick and "snappy." Powerful, direct blocks almost to the point of breaking an arm or leg will be utilized. Punches and kicks are equally direct, linear, and penetrating.

In contrast, a soft system, like tai chi or aikido, places its emphasis on relaxation and suppleness. Movement tends to be flowing and continuous. The principle is not to oppose an attacker's force but to use that incoming force against the attacker himself. Throws or locks will merge with the opponent's momentum to guide him spiralling to the ground. Punches and kicks tend to be more pushes which fling the attacker away.

Another distinction that is often drawn between hard and soft styles is the relative use of the mind. The hard-style approach is also referred to as the external school. This style is more concerned with the use of physical strength and the outer body, although of course there is much mental discipline involved as well. The soft style, or internal school, places a much greater stress on the mind; force is thought to arise more from the very center of the body.

There has been endless controversy over the advantages and disadvantages of each approach and, again, many schools utilize both types of movement. Japanese goju-ryu karate (which means "hard-soft school") and Korean hwarang-do would fall into this category.

The developing American karate tradition is another prime example of the incorporation of both kinds of technique. A full-contact fighter, especially, can be seen slipping blows like a kung fu stylist or boxer, and delivering straight line punches or kicks like a karateka.

A Word about Weapons

Many martial art systems forgo the use of weapons, deciding instead to forge the natural weapons of the human body into the equivalents of clubs and swords. The hard styles, especially, stress development of callouses on the punching knuckles, and some fighters have been known to break the middle finger to shorten it, creating a better alignment of the fingertips for spear-hand strikes. This is not only damaging, as we've previously said, but it is unnecessary, since an unprotected hand can easily break wood or brick, and the human body is certainly more vulnerable than these.

Other systems of martial arts utilize only weapons, such as Japanese kendo (bamboo stick and sword fighting) and Okinawan kobudo ("weapons way"). More frequently, however, a kung fu, karate, or aikido instructor will also incorporate a few weapons techniques into his training. Most teachers reserve weapons instruction for the more advanced students, preferring to perfect more basic empty-hand techniques first. I had the opportunity to work on a very good weapons book with Dr. Ted Gambordella (we'll talk to him later) which I can recommend if you are interested in further studies in this area.*

---

*The Complete Book of Karate Weapons, Dr. Ted Gambordella, Paladin Press.

CHAPTER THREE

The Mental Aspects

The Psychological and Spiritual Dimensions

In recent years Western society has placed a growing emphasis on personal development, self-improvement, and the "maximizing of one's potential." We have the transcendental meditation movement, the assertiveness training movement, est, and on and on. Sometimes they work, according to those most involved, but sometimes they do not. I think it probably depends a lot on the preconceptions and peculiarities of the individuals and what they expect to get out of that activity. Not all people who get involved with martial arts do so for the psychological benefits; in fact, most are not even aware of them. But people who have studied any martial art for more than a few months say there are profound and far-reaching changes that take place in the mind.

Bob Bartlett played professional football for almost five years. He looks like an ex-ball player, big neck and shoulders and a waistline slightly expanded through the absence of two-a-days.

"My karate training helped me mentally prepare for my football," says Bartlett, who was already a black belt by the time he started his pro career. "I started off as the class runt where they literally lined up after school to beat me up. Karate helped change the image I had of myself.

"One of the things I feel the most strongly about the martial arts is the mental discipline it develops. I believe you can do anything you will yourself to do. The martial arts teach this. This whole idea of mind over matter taught me to do breaking techniques, to take physical abuse, and martial arts training *is* physical abuse, and that gave me the extra incentive in my football career. When you think, 'My God, I can't run another wind sprint,' you just put yourself into that frame of mind that says, 'You *can* run another ten yards, you *can* take that tackle.'

"I'm only six one," says the former linebacker, "and when you're out there hitting six six or six eight tackles who are trying to kill you, you've got to mentally prepare yourself. The martial arts teach you that you don't have to be big, you just have to know what to do."

The martial arts, for the most part, do not depend on strength or brute force, but on the use of skill. How to use your body effectively and efficiently is largely a function of the mind.

Tom Seabourne is a past karate champion who has done intensive study on the mental aspects of martial arts training. While working on his master's and doctoral degrees in sports psychology at North Texas State University, he arranged an experiment with four groups of karate students. Seabourne had one group practice relaxation techniques like meditation and deep breathing exercises. He instructed the second group to do what he calls "imagery training."

"The imagery is seeing themselves perform from the internal point of view rather than just watching themselves from a crowd's perspective," Seabourne told me. "By internal I mean that you can see your opponent but you're not able to see yourself." The students were told to visualize themselves fighting better than they had ever done before, blocking everything and scoring with everything they threw.

The third group of students in the experiment combined the meditation and relaxation techniques as well as the visual imaging. The fourth group did neither but were required to memorize ancient Chinese sayings.

The first two groups, the ones using the relaxation methods, were found to be much lower in anxiety levels for their final performance tests. The groups using the visualization techniques were noticeably better in their actual performance of both forms and sparring.

The results of this research have revolutionized the way Seabourne now teaches. He always has his students spend a few minutes in a mini-relaxation/imagery drill where they imagine themselves performing what they are about to do.

Seabourne also uses this method in his self-defense

training. "We tell the students to imagine any situation that could possibly happen, whether they are getting out of their car or walking to their office or whatever. It's important to not just imagine it but to go through it physically too, because it has been found from other studies in sports psychology that mental practice is really only valuable if it is followed by physical practice," he says.

"The mind plays a very big role, not only in arts like karate or judo but in everyday life," says aikido expert Bill Sosa. "We call this proper attitude. This means that we are courteous and respectful and humble. It also means that you will always do your best."

Sosa gave me an example. "Some high-ranking belts wouldn't start another martial art because they would have to put on a white belt again and their egos get in the way. That's not the proper mental attitude. Martial arts are supposed to teach you how to get rid of things like that. They were not developed for competition but for self-defense— for the discipline of the mind and body—for coordination, health, and well-being."

Indeed, the Oriental warrior arts have historically been more than just methods of fighting. They have been deeply involved in the philosophies and religions of the Far East. Many systems were, in fact, developed within a deep framework of religious precepts.

Some instructors, especially those in the internal disciplines, have said that unless you understand these philosophical roots you can never achieve true mastery of the art.

It is because of such claims that evangelical Christian writer Bob Larson has listed martial arts in his *Book of Cults.* Larson maintains that the background of Buddhism and Taoism have made the martial arts a "distinctly pagan" practice that he warns Christians to be careful of.

As he told me, "You can say you'll just learn the techniques and not the philosophy, but some senseis are so subtle

Fig. 9 A drawing based on an old painting shows *Lao Tzu*, a Chinese philosopher who is said to have written the canon of Taoism about 300 B.C. The soft arts of China, hsing-i, pa-kua, and tai chi, are based on his teachings and observations of nature. Taoists distrusted analytical thinking, believing instead that only intuitive insight was needed for an understanding of man and his place in the world. They placed great emphasis on living life in harmony with what they saw to be the natural laws of the universe.

that you never know when they are teaching Zen principles."

Now, whether or not you agree with Larson about Christians being involved with the martial arts, you should know that he is right about their inextricable connection to non-Christian religious philosophies.

Undoubtedly the best example is the concept of ki (or, in Chinese, ch'i). This psychophysical energy plays an important role in most martial systems. Trying to find a precise definition of ki, as I found out, is a rather elusive task. Few can agree on terminology, let alone the actual concept.

Rob Kobiyashi, a Los Angeles aikido master, describes it as the "universal essence of the universe." He says that "everything is made of ki just as everything is made of atoms. Trees, grass, birds, animals, everything has ki."

Dr. John Painter teaches an internal Chinese system he calls *tao ch'i chuan.* He calls ki the "creative life force" of the universe, likening it to the Christian concept of God. He says that ki existed before anything else did and became the force that created all else that we know.

Remember when Luke Skywalker first asked Ben Kenobi in *Star Wars* about the Force? He replied that it was "an energy field that flows around us and through us. It binds the universe together." He might just have well called it ki.

Eastern philosophy teaches that God isn't a personal creator-being that is *in control of the world* (theism) or even a divine being *beyond the world* (deism) but rather God is in the world, or perhaps more accurately, *is the world* (pantheism). God, if you could call him that, in this view, is an impersonal sustaining "force."

These ideas can be traced back to 2696 B.C. and the *I-Ching* or "Book of Changes." Pa-kua, one of the oldest Chinese martial arts, is based on the *I-Ching.* The Chinese sage Lao Tzu (born in 604 B.C.) refined these philosophies in his *Tao Teh Ching,* frequently just called "The Way" or "The Tao."

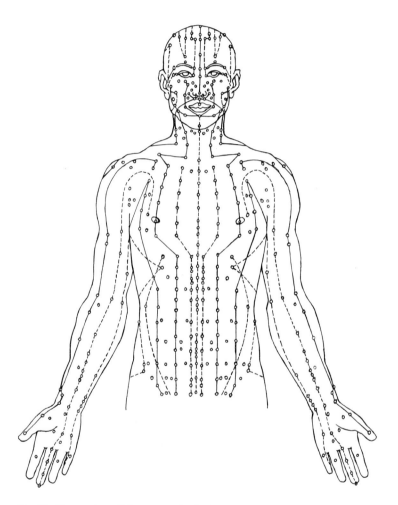

Fig. 10 The ancient Chinese saw the body as balanced between yin and yang, with ch'i (the energy life force) flowing freely through it. Sickness and disease are believed to be caused by imbalance. In acupuncture a needle is inserted into one of the points illustrated here in order to speed up or slow down the energy flow, depending on the diagnosis. The flow always takes certain paths, and so a single needle inserted between the thumb and forefinger, for instance, numbs the mouth for oral surgery. Although dismissed for years by Western experts, hundreds of acupuncture points have now been documented with names like the Golden Gate, Whirlpool, and Soul Door.

It's almost impossible to describe a whole philosophy of life in just a few words, but I'll try. Taoists believe that the Tao is eternal and all-pervasive. Immaterial or spiritual being is not separated from material or physical being. Man is to live his life in harmony with the Tao, staying in tune with the universe, so to speak, and only then can he experience true peace. The fundamental component within the Tao is the energy flow of ch'i (ki).

Acupuncture is based on this concept of ki flow. There are supposedly certain spots that, when probed by a needle, will either restrict or promote the flow of ch'i through a person's body. The classical Chinese warrior arts utilize these same vital points not only for healing purposes but for stunning and even killing an opponent.

A knowledge of these vital points is only one aspect of the connection between ki and the martial arts. The practice of the internal arts such as hsing-i, pa-kua, tai chi, and aikido is aimed at exercising the flow of ki throughout the entire body. Ki is thought to be centered in the human body at a point about three inches below the navel called the *hara* *(tan-tien* in Chinese). One of the ways to strengthen the ki is through meditation exercises.

Za-Zen is the seated meditation of Zen Buddhism. Zen differs from other sects of Buddhism in that it teaches that one can attain enlightenment or a "state of oneness" *(satori)* not in future lives, but here and now in this life. The way to do this is through intense meditation and the cultivation of the sense of intuition. Zen teachers frequently pose unanswerable questions to their pupils like, "What is the sound of one hand clapping?" These *koans* are not meant to make the student think, for no answer can come from rational, logical thought. They are meant to stimulate. Zen takes as its prime concern the concept of emptiness. The mind is to be completely open and free, taking in everything without effort and without distortion. At this point mind, body, and spirit are to be in complete harmony. This is known as *mushin,* or no-mind. At the highest level of no-mind, the martial arts master is supposed to be able to fend off his opponents effortlessly and, according to some, without any physical contact at all.

Now, I have to admit that as a hard-style tae kwon-do martial artist learning under American instructors, I had very little exposure to these esoteric aspects of the Oriental warrior arts during most of my training. Most Americans, in fact, know very little about and think very little of these ideas of ki energy and contemplative meditation to empty the mind. They teach the fighting arts in physical and mental terms, to be sure, but they leave out the so-called spiritual side. As one well-known karate fighter told me, "Ki is a religious concept, and I don't think you have to be religious in order to be a good martial artist."

"We are playing with words here," says kung fu teacher John Painter. "I mean, what is a martial art? To some people

Fig. 11 World full-contact champion Raymond McCallum shows the meditation posture he uses in his training routine.

it is a .357 magnum. To some people it means being able to kick somebody's face in and in that respect, yes, you can get into martial arts without [knowing about ki] although the word 'art' wouldn't really apply there. There's no art in breaking a man's face. There's no art in breaking someone's ribs. There's no art in shooting someone. We might say martial mayhem, yes, but martial art, no."

Besides teaching his style of tao ch'i chuan, Painter claims to instruct his students in psychic healing, or "therapeutic touch." He holds a doctorate in naturo-pathology, the science of healing with herbs instead of with medicines.

"Most *external* martial arts, and by that I am talking about Shaolin styles and karate and so on, have concepts of ki or ch'i," says Painter. "But the internal martial arts, which include aikido in Japan, and tai chi chuan, pa-kua chang, and hsing-i, are based solely, completely, wholly on ch'i, and to practice one of them without going into meditation and without understanding yourself and without developing an inner goodness or holiness, if you will, is very much like having a pie with only the shell and nothing else.

"To me, a real martial art, and I don't really like the word 'martial' very much," continues Painter, "is one that makes a whole integrated human being. In the Orient we had a system which, for the person practicing it, produced a philosophical way of thinking, produced an awareness of body, produced an awareness of mind, and eventually produced an awareness of something beyond that, spirit.

"But Americans are so compartmentalized in their outlook. They want their karate over here, their guns over here, their ministers over here, and they just took what they wanted and threw the rest away. A lot of the masters say the martial arts in this country, as far as their true purpose is concerned, have been totally watered down and they are nothing more than a wooden dance. Oh, it's possible to create havoc with someone's body once in a while, but there's nothing there to help them spiritually."

Even though I agree with Dr. Painter that the martial arts are not practiced with the same disposition in America as in the Orient, I still believe that there are benefits which extend beyond the purely physical when you are fortunate enough to train with a competent and dedicated instructor. Whether these benefits can be called psychological or spiritual depends on the perspective of the individual.

Much of our lives are spent in subservience to others— bosses, government officials, even mothers-in-law. Our need for self-assertion is always being forced back. Martial arts practice gives us a way of asserting ourselves, of being competitive either with ourselves (in some non-competitive arts like tai chi or aikido) or with others (as in judo or karate). Ideally, this controlled way of self-assertion will even produce a sense of humility as you get better and better.

Americans are into winning. We tend to think that it is good to win and bad to lose. But no matter how good you are, you occasionally lose. Martial arts change our attitudes toward defeat. Even when we spar, we are competing not so much against the other person as against ourselves. If we win, great, but if we lose—well, that's okay too, because hopefully we have learned something about ourselves in the process. Now I know that all coaches tend to preach that same message. "By swimming, by playing football, by dancing, you will become a better person," and so on. I just think that in the martial arts it is a greater part of the basic philosophy.

If you are like me, you find that your life often seems undisciplined. If only you could set goals and then see yourself accomplish them. Even if it was hard work you wouldn't mind—you would experience the satisfaction of a coordinated effort between mind (what you set out to do) and body (what you really do). Bruce Lee was right when he said

"Martial arts training gives you goals and then the skills and confidence to attain those goals."

I'm a pretty busy guy. Besides writing books and articles I work a fifty- to sixty-hour week as a graphic designer. I've got three small children and I'm active in my local church. When I get to my martial arts class (I'm currently teaching a tae kwon-do class and taking an aikido class), I've got so much on my mind that it is often difficult to concentrate. Once I bow in, though, all other thoughts and problems seem to disappear. I am free to stretch, to sweat, to, in a sense, play like a child again. I'm convinced that martial arts, and probably most other forms of physical exercise as well, will keep you young at heart.

Let's not leave out one of the most important benefits of training, and that is self-confidence. Even though, for the most part, martial arts teach the concept of nonviolent self-defense, such as talk your way out, turn and run, and so on, there is something to be said for having the knowledge that you could really deck someone if you had to. This feeling of self-confidence carries over into other areas of life besides the dojo (school). When you feel better about yourself and your abilities, you are able to function a little bit better in your job, your school, your relationships with other people. By building your confidence level you can begin to set other goals that were previously unthinkable. This is why I think martial arts training is especially good for children and young adolescents who are struggling with feelings of inferiority and lack of self-confidence.

I'm going to finish this chapter with a final observation. Not only are there many different styles of martial arts, there are many different styles of instructors. Not all teachers emphasize the same qualities. If you are interested in certain aspects of martial arts training, like the mental aspects, talk to the teacher. Talk also to the students. Find out what the classes are like. If you expect a spiritual encounter when you sign up at a school that emphasizes full-contact fighting—the only way you'll get it is when they knock you out! If you're like most people, you just want to learn how to defend yourself effectively, and you wouldn't mind gaining more self-confidence and getting physically fit in the bargain. The vast majority of martial arts schools can do that and much more for you.

CHAPTER FOUR

Modern Karate and Tae Kwon·Do

The Americanization of Karate

Over twenty years ago I walked into my first karate class. I fully expected to be able to break boards and bricks by my third lesson, and I knew no one in junior high school would ever call me skinny again. In the years since I have matured and so has my art. Karate schools then were usually nothing more than four walls and a mirror or two. The first school I taught in wasn't even air conditioned (a real torture in the Texas summers). Today there are luxurious martial arts centers replete with universal gyms, saunas, whirlpools, wall-to-wall mats and, yes, central air conditioning. Because the training facilities are so much improved, the athletes are naturally much better conditioned and, I think, much more skilled in their variety and use of techniques. As a result, the beginning student of today is much better off than even ten years ago.

This contemporary method of teaching the ancient arts has evolved quickly in the United States. As I mentioned in chapter one, karate really only came to this country after World War II. Robert Trias is credited with opening the nation's first dojo (school) in 1946, in Phoenix, Arizona. Ed Parker, the famous California kempo master and "teacher of the stars," opened his first school in 1956. By 1960 many major cities had their own karate or tae kwon-do schools, usually started by a newly arrived Oriental seeking his fortune in America. For those first few years karate remained very traditional in its approach, but by the mid-sixties what East Coast instructor Dr. Jerry Beasley calls the "progressive era" of American karate had arrived.

Many American instructors resented the Orientals for wanting to perpetuate the "purity" of the art and for wanting to prevent the Westerners from introducing any "deviations" into their traditions. Americans felt that the only way to keep karate evolving was to be open to intermingling with other systems, something the traditionalists had a hard time accepting.

"America is the karate capital of the world because it

has fulfilled the original dream of karate for all people, due to the many open tournaments and the core of multi-racial sensei. America (therefore) has superior karate technology . . . ," says Peter Urban in a recent interview in *Kick Illustrated* magazine. In 1960, Urban formed his *American goju* system in New York City and declared himself this country's first native tenth degree black belt, an act that outraged his Oriental teachers.

But Urban was typical of a growing number of Americans to take a pragmatic—if it works, use it—approach, even if others didn't have the nerve to start their own styles. Another early instructor who also organized his own American style, based on a variety of techniques, was Salt Lake City sensei Mickey Fisher.

Fisher grew up in the early days of karate in the Southwest. His first training was in the hard-kicking Korean style of tae kwon-do. He admits that he thought his style was the best and the toughest, and that he even used to laugh at the competitors from other systems.

Says Fisher, "I even said to Ed Parker, when I was at one of his early tournaments when I was a green belt, that he was all flash, and then he gave me a personal demonstration wherein I changed my mind. We became friends and Mr. Parker spent some time working with me."

Parker's Chinese kempo karate was known for its quick, fluid hand techniques as opposed to the strong-legged kicks of tae kwon-do. During Fisher's exposure to the Chinese hand methods, he started questioning the proficiency of his own Korean system hand training.

"I felt I could do anything with my feet but I wondered if I got caught in a situation, like under a table or something, if I even knew as much as a good Golden Gloves boxer." So Fisher followed the pattern of many early American karate-kas and started working out in other styles, such as shorin-ryu, to widen his variety of hand techniques.

"I wanted to experiment around but I didn't want to

be known as a rebel stylist and I didn't want to call myself tae kwon-do or kempo either," Fisher told me. "So I legitimized it [his style] in 1964, by giving it a name and logo. *Shin* means 'new way' and *toshi* means 'eclectic.' So it is a kind of an East/West combination, along the same lines of Bruce Lee's jeet kune do."

Bruce Lee was perhaps the most well-known nontraditionalist by the general public although ironically most of his non-martial arts followers never knew how he rebelled against the traditional way of doing things. His background was Chinese wing chun but his own, original system, *jeet kune do,* rejected what Lee called the "sterile" classical moves in favor of an amalgamated technique of time-proven Oriental ideas combined with much of Western boxing and wrestling.

Dan Inosanto is a widely respected instructor *(Black Belt* magazine's 1983 "Instructor of the Year"), best-selling author, and one of Bruce Lee's first students.

"Bruce wasn't the first one necessarily to amalgamate systems," says Inosanto, "but I'd say he was the first one in the public eye to profess to that kind of philosophy. He came from a background of northern kung fu which used a lot of kicking. In Hong Kong he did a lot of trading techniques with other systems. Additionally he was greatly influenced by Western boxing. He studied it in detail and used to say that there were a lot of different styles in boxing and was amazed that more people weren't influenced by it. As early as 1964 he said that if there was ever full-contact karate, then people are going to find out that their hands are inadequate and they're going to have to go to boxing trainers to develop and reeducate their hands. And that's basically true," Dan told me. "Most of the better ones in full contact, from Urquidez to Wallace, have gotten boxing trainers to help them.

"Bruce liked French savate and incorporated some of that into his training. He liked what the Thai kick boxers did and also thought the various elements of *kali* (an Indonesian fighting art) were very good. He felt it shouldn't be named. He said that when you are confined within a certain structure you tend to try and solve all your problems from within the compounds of that structure.

"His first group in Chinatown was made up of people from various disciplines, like tae kwon-do, tai chi chuan, shotokan. We came under him because he was saying things we all wanted to say but didn't dare to because we would offend a lot of people. We were a maverick group, because in those days the Chinese were very clicquish and their art wouldn't be taught to anyone outside their group. They didn't like Bruce because he was the first one to take it to non-Chinese," says Inosanto.

Lee considered his art ever-changing; each concept was in a constant state of evolution. He constantly experimented with new techniques and was always improving on them. His martial arts and movie careers were just taking off when cut short by his premature death in 1973.

That same year the first Korean World Tae Kwon-Do Championships were held in Seoul, Korea. The United States team finished second, a feat surprising to the Koreans. One of the star members of the American contingent was James Butin, who considered himself a traditionalist at the time. I'll let him tell the story.

"When I got there and started competing in a 'pure' tae kwon-do system and we had to abide by *their* rules, I found that the things that I used here, like sweeps, knees, hand techniques to the face, [and] kicking to the groin, were illegal in Korea. So I said, 'Wait a minute, I say I'm teaching tae kwon-do, but the things I teach—things that work—are illegal here. So why am I in the U.S.A. waving the Korean flag [and] claiming the superiority of the tae kwon-do system when what we're teaching is not really tae kwon-do?"

Butin credits his incredibly powerful kicks to his early Korean-style training, but says that what he teaches now in his Oklahoma City dojo is "American karate." He has toured the entire country, competing successfully in almost every major tournament, and also fought in Europe alongside the likes of Jeff Smith, Howard Jackson, Joe Lewis, and Bill Wallace.

"In those days," says Butin, "we were developing whatever was useful. I didn't realize it at the time, but after reading some of Bruce Lee's concepts about experimenting with what works and developing your own style . . . that's what we were doing.

"A lot of guys still say they are teaching tae kwon-do, but they really aren't," says Butin. "They just haven't had the opportunity to make the comparisons I have. As an American, I'm going to do a technique because of its effect rather than its origin. If a boxer hits me with a jab, I'm going to say, 'Hey, that's pretty swift.' If a shotokan stylist sweeps me, I'm going to say, 'Wow, I was off-balance and that guy did it to me,' and there's value in that! We've been developing a conglomerate system in this country for years now."

Amalgamation of systems notwithstanding, there are still discernible differences in the approach of certain various traditions. We spoke at length about that in chapter two, but let me just say an additional word specifically about variations within the arts classified as "karate."

I caution you to realize that any distinctions in the many styles of karate are often blurred by this "Americanization" process we have been talking about. One school that teaches Okinawan shorin-ryu, for example, could easily be teaching a slightly different approach than another shorin-ryu dojo across town because that instructor might have studied some Korean tang soo do somewhere along the line.

Nevertheless, we can divide the styles of karate into four broad categories: Japanese, Okinawan, Korean, and Chinese. Of course, technically, karate is a Japanese word meaning "empty hand" but it has come to be a catch-all term includ-

Fig. 12 In Okinawan karate the *sanchin* kata is performed with gi tops off so that muscular tension can be seen. Sanchin deep breathing is to be done with the abdomen and all the other muscles tightened. Correct posture and stances are also important.

ing any of the karatelike arts no matter what their country of origin.

Japanese and Okinawan styles are so close that only a discerning and experienced eye can detect any difference. Japanese systems generally have lower and wider stances than Okinawan styles. This affords them better solidity and complements their aggressive approach to fighting. They especially like grabs and sweeping techniques.

The typical Okinawan stylist, by contrast, adopts a position of greater mobility, usually by standing more upright, and relies less on constant forward pressure of his opponent. He is more elusive than his Japanese counterpart, generally using lower kicks and fast hand techniques.

Actually Okinawan and Japanese karate probably differ more in their approach than in their actual techniques. The Japanese have stressed the competition aspects, while the Okinawans seem content to spend the bulk of their time in more traditional training methods such as kata.

Korean tae kwon-do is perhaps best known for its high and flashy kicks and for hard blocks executed with a maximum body motion. Punches are usually delivered in a straight line; circular or spinning kicks, again, with lots of body momentum, are common. As I've said before, tae kwon-do is a uniquely Korean art and is not really a form of karate. Many Korean masters have traveled to this country to set up their own schools (almost any city of reasonable size has a tae kwon-do school listed in its Yellow Pages) and this system of fighting has begun to establish an identity of its own. It will surely be more widely recognized as distinct from Okinawan or Japanese karate when tae kwon-do is publicized as being only the second martial art to be admitted to the Olympics (judo has long been an Olympic sport). Until then, however, I and many other Occidental tae kwon-do instructors will probably continue to put "karate lessons" on our business cards for easier recognition from the general public.

Although there are Chinese styles of karate or karatelike arts as well, I'm going to reserve most of my observations on the Chinese approach for the chapter on kung fu. In spite of repeated requests for an answer to the question of which style is better, I can't get any more specific than this because there are too many variables to consider. Basically it boils down to this—it doesn't matter which system you take up! I believe that if you are a good athlete, or, for that matter, even if you aren't, if you have a desire to learn and the patience to stick with it, you'll do well. I'm assuming, of course, that you'll be able to find a competent instructor.

There are several ways to judge an instructor. Watch him teach and observe how he communicates to the students. (Incidentally, be wary of a school that won't let you watch a class.) Some black belts run their classes like Marine drill sergeants. Others take a more low-key approach.

Fig. 13 A forward stance is very powerful from front to rear and also stable from side to side. The weak point is the 45 degree angle. Attacks or throws from this angle are much more difficult to defend against.

Bob Bartlett, former pro football player and long-time instructor says, "An instructor is kind of like a coach. Look closely at who you are going to take karate from because you will find yourself becoming like that instructor. If he's a strong kicker, you will be a strong kicker. If he's arrogant and has no respect, you will be arrogant and have no respect."

I asked Mark Shuper, the editor of the popular martial arts magazine, *Inside Karate,* what he tells people who ask him to recommend a school.

"We get calls and letters all the time from people wanting us to recommend a school or style. Our standard editorial reply is simply that we don't recommend schools. We don't ask for people's credentials or for them to demonstrate their abilities. That's not our place. I would tell people, however, to look up some past articles we've done on selecting schools."

I asked Mark if he could give me some guidelines.

"Well, shop around in your area. Visit some different schools and be sure to interview the chief instructor," said Shuper. "It's our experience that the instructor is just as interested in finding out about the prospective student (his background and skills) as the student is in finding out about him. Attend a class and work out with them, if possible; but remember that is a real privilege. What it comes down to is you're the best judge of what you're seeking and whether a particular school fulfills—or will fulfill—your specific needs."

Some people ask how they can tell whether a certain instructor is legitimate. Rank certificates have become a controversial issue because there are no regulated quality controls in karate. Contrary to some claims to be the "official" recognizing association for all of Japanese karate or "American-style" tae kwon-do, there simply is no such body. There are some big and legitimate organizations, to be sure (the United States Karate Association and the World Tae Kwon-

Do Federation, for example), and I'd certainly ask about a school's affiliations. But every one of them has its own sets of rules, regulations, requirements, and prejudices.

In commercial karate schools in America you will invariably start out as a white belt (beginner level). In Japanese karate, ranks below black belt are called *kyu,* meaning "grade." In Korean martial arts the term is *gup.* A white belt is automatically a tenth gup (ninth or eighth in some schools). From there you progress usually to yellow or orange (advanced beginner); to blue, green or purple (intermediate); and then to brown, or in some Korean styles, red belt (advanced intermediate). First gup, or kyu, is just below first *dan,* or degree, black belt. Length of time from belt to belt varies, but it is generally acknowledged that the prescribed period for earliest achievement of the first degree black belt is three years. Because of the great variety of styles, it is difficult to say that absolutely everyone goes through these exact colors, but they are the most common.

In most systems, fifth to ninth degree black belts are honorary promotions where no actual physical testing is required. These ranks are based on length of study and outstanding contribution to the art of karate. In some Japanese schools the color of the belt turns to red and white checked or red with a white stripe at eighth dan. The tenth degree black belt, the highest rank, is reserved for the grandmaster of the styles and is passed on to the master's protegé at his death.

Belt examinations vary, but usually consist of a physical demonstration of basics, *katas* (the prearranged sequences of offensive and defensive techniques), and free-sparring. Some instructors also require a written exam. Again, there are no overall accepted guidelines for determining abilities. Each school and each organization makes up its own rules.

In a recent issue of *Black Belt* magazine, for example, there were five ads inviting people to join various martial arts organizations. The fees ranged from $12 to $200 (but for that one you did get a full-color poster of the founder!). Each of these ads promised to send you a recognized certificate of rank. All you had to do was tell them what art you wanted your black belt in!

"I can make no defense of the ads you see in some of the magazines," says editor Shuper. "It's always been that way and it always will be.

"There are benefits of being in an organization," Shuper is quick to point out, however. "With a large, tightly-run association there are often fairly well-enforced standards. Some are interested in introducing positive innovations into the sport with officially sponsored tournaments and standardized instructional programs."

Since Shuper has had close contact with many of today's leading martial artists, I asked him if he ever saw any possibility of the various organizations and styles getting together under a unified American banner. "None whatsoever," he answered unhesitatingly. "But," he added, "I see that as neither bad nor good. That just goes right along with the history of the martial arts. In the feudal era of Japan, for instance, there was an incredible proliferation of schools and styles and we see that still today.

"In America karate has become a sport. Some of the older practitioners don't care as much for that approach," says Shuper. "They would place the physical and spiritual benefits first with the sporting aspects secondary. But because human beings are different there will always be different approaches and thus a proliferation of styles and organizations."

In a country preoccupied with professional basketball, football, auto-racing, and even table tennis, it was only natural that Americans would invent "professional" karate. Jim Butin has sponsored several Professional Karate Association matches in Oklahoma City and was himself the first challenger for the full-contact world light-heavyweight title when he fought Jeff Smith in Washington, D.C., in 1975. "There is no comparison between then and now," Jim told me. "There was an open platform where now we have rings and boxing gloves. Today, fighters are in better shape and they're better skillwise, using boxing training to augment their karate hand techniques."

One of the men responsible for these kinds of improvements in professional full-contact karate is Joe Corley, noted instructor, competitor, promoter, and one of the founders of the Professional Karate Association. "Full-contact is a different sport (from traditional karate)," Corley told me. "It's a sport that combines boxing and karate. You can see that by the boxing gloves. Our techniques are different than karate hand moves."

But being a full-contact promoter, I wanted to know what Corley teaches in his own Atlanta school. "American

Fig. 14 In today's point karate and full-contact tournaments, competitors are required to wear foam rubber hand and foot guards to prevent serious injuries from the potentially lethal karate blows.

karate" was the answer. "American karate," said Corley, "is
taking some of the principles learned in full-contact and
applying them to karate and self-defense without boxing
gloves on. American karate is *not* full-contact but traditional
karate, improved, updated, twentieth-centuryized. None of
the principles thought to be true when karate was first originated are still believed today. We know the world is not flat
and the earth is not the center of the universe, so why should
bringing one's fist back to the hip be the most powerful way
to punch? We know that's not true," said Corley. "Since we
know it's not true, we have made it better and more realistic.
When a student comes in he is getting what we believe is the
most realistic way of doing it at that point. That doesn't
mean it's not going to change; in fact, that's one of the
things about American karate: the more we learn, the more
we change and the further we get from the traditional way of
doing things. We take anything that will work and apply it."

I asked Joe, who is also an ESPN-TV commentator, about
the reaction of the strict traditionalists to these seemingly
rebel ideas.

"The traditionalists were offended by it initially for the
same reasons that I was a traditionalist for so long," Corley
told me. "Most of us got into the arts because of a basic
insecurity and we found that security in karate. Tradition
provides security. You have these hundreds of years of security and once someone begins to question that, they are, in
a way, questioning your security. But once you have a sense
of security in yourself you can begin to question the traditional more. One of the ways you feel secure is to see that
Joe Corley, for instance, challenged tradition and he didn't
die and he didn't go bankrupt and that his students are still
okay, so maybe I can go outside the little shell I've built
around myself. The bottom line is that the traditionalists are
no longer offended. They now know they can make a choice
and look at American karate and traditional karate, and if

Fig. 15 Roy D. Kurban was one of America's premier karate competitors during the 1970s. He was ranked in the top ten fighters in the U.S.A. for five straight years and in the top ten in the world for two years. *Karate Illustrated* magazine named him the Outstanding Tournament Referee in the United States in both 1980 and 1983. *Official Karate* magazine named him Man of the Decade in 1980 and the *Black Belt* magazine Hall of Fame lists him alongside the likes of Bruce Lee, Chuck Norris, and Bill Wallace. Mr. Kurban trained for a year under Master Park Won Chik in Seoul, Korea, and is one of the few Americans to hold a Master Instructor Certificate from the World Tae Kwon-Do Federation. He currently is the chief referee for the Karate International Council of Kickboxing.

Kurban notes a fundamental difference in his American training vs. his Korean training. "In Korea the training was aimed at developing the entire person more than just self-defense ability as in most training in the United States," he says. "They seemed more interested in the development of the individual as a human being. The Koreans have more of a wholistic approach than the American eclectic systems which stress mainly physical results."

Perhaps it is Kurban's exposure to this kind of training that has made him what many believe to be the "gentleman of karate."

they decide to stick with traditional karate it's because they've looked at both sides and decided they liked it better."

George Chung, called by *Karate Illustrated* magazine "the most creative and flashy forms performer on the circuit," is a prime example of a traditional stylist turning to a modern approach.

"I come out of an extremely traditional tae kwon-do background," George told me. "Although my mother is Japanese and my father Korean, my lifestyle growing up was not a traditional Oriental lifestyle, so I guess my way of thinking is not that traditional. My training was very traditional, however, with a Korean instructor. But there comes a time when you leave your instructor and you have to ask, 'Am I going to do it his way or am I going to do it my way and possibly make it better?'"

There is no doubt that George has done it his way. Doing his forms to the "Star Wars" theme or some contemporary rock hit, Chung cartwheels and flips through the air in his flamboyant journey to the top spot in almost every kata competition he enters. *Black Belt* magazine named him "Competitor of the Year" for 1983 and *Karate Illustrated* placed him at the top of their 1983 National Forms Competitor Ratings. He believes in the traditional values of the martial arts but has added what he called "American ingenuity."

"American karate is a generic term," explains Chung. "It says we are doing something different. For years all the styles bickered with each other saying, 'My style is better than yours.' Well, the American contribution has been to say that we are all going to work together which is going to, one, make us more money, two, get bigger turnouts at tournaments, and three, make a potpourri of styles and systems that together make a better art."

Even those who still have a traditional reputation can be seen to be evolving and changing because of the Western influence. Jhoon Rhee is considered the father of tae kwon-do in the United States, being the first man to teach it in this country in the late 1950s. He now runs a highly successful chain of schools from his Washington, D.C., headquarters. Mr. Rhee, who was my instructor's instructor, was *Black Belt* magazine's "Man of the Year" for 1983. He had not been in this country for very long before he realized what the Americans wanted from the martial arts and began applying his ingenuity to this new problem. He is the man who invented the first protective foam karate sparring pads and now teaches what his nephew and the number one traditional kata competitor in the United States, John Chung (no relation to George), calls an "Americanized form of traditional tae kwon-do."

Chung, an instructor in one of Rhee's East Coast schools as well as a competitor, says their style of teaching is traditional, yet contemporary. He gave me an example:

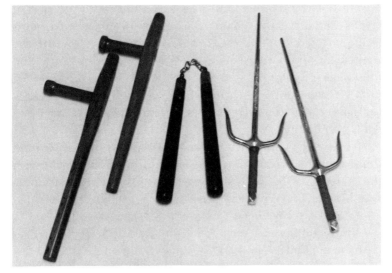

Fig. 16 Some of the weapons you will see in karate practice are the wooden *tonfa*, the *nunchuku*, which can be connected with either a rope or a chain, and the *sai*, a short sword used by peasants to defend themselves against the samurai.

"The traditional way to kick is with the supporting leg bent ... but by bending the leg you are getting less extension and less thrust and even less balance. So we kick with a straight supporting leg. This is one way we are changing the system. We are not changing into an American style and forgetting the traditional," said Chung, "but Mr. Rhee has very much adapted to a Western (way of thinking)."

John had a word of warning to add to those seeking a contemporary American style. "I see many schools saying they are an American style," said Chung, "but you can still see their origins—Korean, Japanese, Chinese, et cetera. They may concentrate a little more on fighting and they get an easy way out by not having to do all the basic stances and stuff. And they don't get all the artistic value either. If they do it properly it is good for the sport, but there are so many out just for the quick buck—opening and closing quickly— that it gives a bad name to the martial arts."

One of the schools that gives a good name to the martial arts is the successful chain of Mid-American karate schools headquartered in Minnesota. Larry Carnahan is one of the chain's owners besides being a well-known point-karate and full-contact fighter.

"I teach sparring with a full-contact emphasis," Larry told me. "We use different kicks and our hands are more related to boxing."

To watch a class in the Mid-American school you would think you are witnessing a more traditional approach, with the training forms and all. But forms *are* good for training and besides, as Carnahan says with a twinkle, "you must know where you've been to know where you're going."

"Full-contact is separate from karate," acknowledges Carnahan. "I'm in the karate business, not the fighting business. Lawyers and doctors don't want full-contact. Fighting is, after all, only a small part of karate. You don't need to know how to spar in order to defend yourself, although of course a good fighter will be able to."

Is it true that you don't have to be a fighter to be able to defend yourself? Mid-America's most famous fighter, John Longstreet, agrees. "A street situation will last no more than a few seconds and there are no rules," emphasizes Longstreet.

John made the transition from a top-point fighter to full-contact fighter in 1981 in impressive style. *Karate Illustrated* magazine rated him number five in the nation in 1982. He admits there is a big mental difference between amateur tournaments and full-contact. In a point-match, "you are in it more for the knowledge, the experience, et cetera," he told me, "but in full-contact there is a mental emphasis; you train to knock out your opponent."

But oddly enough, Longstreet believes that "a traditional fighter has an advantage in a street situation because the full-contact fighter can sometimes forget he is in a real situation and forget to use his knees, his elbows, groin kicks, and other techniques [which are outlawed in the full-contact ring]."

Roy Kurban, another well-known competitor and promoter, echoes the same sentiments. "In full-contact you train more for endurance or stamina, whereas in more traditional karate you are practicing primarily for a self-defense application." Traditional karate self-defense has a wider variety of techniques, such as eye gouges and joint kicks, believes Kurban. "But," he says, "the full-contact fighter understands pain, which can be vitally important in a life-or-death situation."

Mark Shuper had much the same sentiments, stating that in a more traditional approach like Japanese shotokan or some Okinawan systems there is a rich history of "essential fighting theory." He believes that a greater variety of techniques, like knees and elbows for close-range defense, better prepares a person for that once-in-a-lifetime situation. Tournament fighting looks exciting and effective because of the flashy techniques, while some of the more traditional stylists doing their forms in the kata competition might look stilted and confined. But don't be misled, insists Shuper. Those long-honored techniques can be very effective. He cites goju-ryu as a style that looks very esoteric with its breathing exercises and short movements but one that can be quite deadly in a self-defense situation.

I remember the day a wide-eyed student came into class telling me how he had successfully defended himself that very weekend. He was a drummer in a little band and between sets at the local honky-tonk was at the bar chatting with an attractive blond. Suddenly he was spun around by a large drunk, wielding an even larger looking knife, demanding that he stop talking to "his girl." Before my friend realized what was going on, the ruffian had lunged at him with the knife. My student instinctively came around with a roundhouse kick to the floating ribs. His attacker went down like the proverbial lead balloon. It wasn't until later, after my student had quickly exited the bar, that he realized he had actually been cut. Fortunately it wasn't severe, and there he was only hours later relating his story.

One of the things that made me marvel was that this guy was not a brown belt or even a blue belt but a lowly orange belt, and not a particularly adept one at that. Yet, with just one basic technique he had done what many karate students dream of doing, dropping a real-life attacker. Even though that was several years ago, I still constantly remind my students of the effectiveness of basic techniques.

"Self-defense techniques themselves haven't changed much over the years," states Fred Wren, a highly successful St. Louis instructor and five-time *Black Belt* magazine top ten fighter who started his championship career way back in 1963. "But the fighting we do in the school has changed since the early days because of the emphasis on full-contact competition." Wren also believes that this has helped, "not the self-defense techniques themselves but in their practical application to street fighting.

"After you release yourself from an attacker's grab," Fred told me, "You are either going to be running or fighting. No matter how good you are, you are probably going to be hit, and sparring, especially in the competitive manner it is taught today, prepares you to take that hit." Wren takes a very practical approach in his 5,000 square foot, fully equipped St. Louis dojo. He teaches karate on three different levels—art, sport, and self-defense—but he recognizes that most people want to learn self-defense.

"I really don't think that the full-contact movement has influenced any more people to come in and sign up. Most of our students simply want to learn how to defend themselves." And Wren, like most instructors, has found that the best path to that end is the basic one.

Roy Kurban's approach to self-defense is also a basic and practical one. "We teach a beginner just a few techniques but we want him to be able to do them very well. Jump back kicks and the like aren't even shown to them until green or blue belt level. In that sense I stick to a traditional, basic style of karate," says *Black Belt* magazine's 1981 "Man of the Year."

And that practical approach to self-defense has served Kurban personally.

"When I was in the army I had to use my karate in several situations," he remembers. "You know, in the five or six times that I did, it never lasted more than one punch or kick. We trained to knock out an opponent with one technique. I have *never* had to use a combination," he told me. "I side kicked a guy in the solar plexus once and he went right down. I've used front kicks to the groin and a lunge punch and they've always ended the fight right off. Now, maybe I

was just lucky, or just got weak opponents, but I don't think
so. I've got tremendous confidence in very basic, and strong,
self-defense techniques."

The number two rated fighter in the United States for
1983 says the same thing. Raymond McCallum told me that
his basic theory of self-defense is "basic karate techniques."

"In the magazines," says McCallum, "you see a lot of
stuff that isn't all that realistic. I mean if they ask someone to do self-defense techniques and he just goes front
kick punch, they'll say 'Big deal, why should we put that
in a magazine?'" Raymond picks up a recent copy of one of
the magazines off his desk for an example. He flips a few
pages and starts reading. "'Grip the inside of the knife hand
and execute a forearm strike with the left while pulling forward.'" McCallum adds, "Now he breaks this guy's arm in
three places!

"If I was in that situation and a guy had a knife on me I
would use a long-range technique; I wouldn't be trying to
grasp him and pull him in closer to me. Now, if he had a
gun, I would try to get as close as possible to him, but knives
are something you don't want to get too close to. You either
avoid the situation or kick him in the shin or break his leg so
he can't chase you. Even with an empty hand attack if someone is bigger than you are, just a simple side kick to the knee
would finish him off instead of all this grabbing and takedowns and stuff."

I asked Ray if he ever had to use his training.

"Not in a long while," he replied. "But every fight I've
been in since I was a black belt has been just a front kick
punch or even a simple reverse punch." He gave me an
example.

It's hard to believe someone would pick a fight with the
World Karate Association middleweight champion, but,
McCallum said, "I was in a club with a friend of mine right
around Christmastime and I had gone into the restroom.

Fig. 17 Thirteen-year martial arts veteran, *Ismael Robles,* is the K.I.C.K. World Welterweight Full-Contact Karate Champion and the U.S. Champion in both the P.K.A. and the W.K.A. He says that full-contact is a totally different sport than traditional karate. "It's like comparing flag football to tackle football. The public needs to be educated that what they see on ESPN is not 'karate,' it's 'full-contact' and there's a world of difference between the two," Robles says. Because of his boxing background Ismael was naturally drawn to full-contact. "I like the intense training and conditioning you need. It's like going from a two-mile run to a marathon. I feel that no traditional point fighter can say he trains as hard as me or do as well as me [in the ring]," he claims. In spite of Robles' affinity for full-contact, he still teaches traditional tae kwon-do in his Galveston, Texas school. "Most people want to learn self-defense and I think that the traditional approach is better for that. Most full-contact fighters probably would be trying to go for a KO in the street instead of doing knee kicks or something like that," he says.

Robles trains for an upcoming title defense on the speed bag. "Bag work is good for your timing and coordination," he says. "You can develop more rhythm on a bag than on an actual opponent and rhythm is important to your combinations. It usually takes a good one-two or one-two-three combination to get in a knockout punch."

There was this big drunk standing there wrapping toilet paper around his fist saying to me, 'watch me break this mirror.' So I told him to calm down 'cause it was Christmas and everything, but he just said, 'No, I'm going to break it and *you're* going to watch me.' As he reached out to shove me I just punched him in the face once and he went down like lead. I just stepped over him and walked on out."

Indeed, most street fights don't last very long if you know basic techniques. As I interviewed several experienced karateka I kept coming up with the same answer:

"That fancy stuff is okay for TV but in the street I'll do basic self-defense every time," says James Toney, a high ranking black belt and one of my own first instructors. "The throat is a prime target area—after all if he can't breathe he can't bother you," says Toney.

"There are many ways to attack the throat too. Perhaps the best is the open-hand strike, sliding up the breastbone and finishing with a pinch where the fingers meet behind the Adam's apple. A hammer fist or chop works well too," Jim continues, "especially if you're to the side where you can get some body into it." I wanted to know if Toney had ever had to use a throat strike in a real situation. "Yeah," he replied, "and I can tell you it really works."

There are many other types of basic karate self-defense techniques that are extremely effective. Joint kicks, eye gouges, and groin strikes are all commonly taught. Such techniques may seem dirty but, as Toney says, "you don't want to stand there and duke it out with a younger, stronger opponent. Self-defense should be a natural reaction where you go to the weakest spot with your best technique and get it over as quickly as you can."

Some people call karate *the* most effective martial art in a street fight. I'm not ready to make that unequivocal a statement, but karate certainly has a more direct method of attack than some of the other arts.

"Wrist locks and holds can be effective, but you have to be pretty proficient with them and that takes time," says Toney. "I can teach you a front kick to the groin or a throat strike in one lesson and you'll be able to use it effectively." Barry Guimbellot, a black belt in both tae kwon-do and ju-jutsu, agrees.

"The meditation and relaxation practice that go along with arts like aikido and ju-jutsu are harder for Americans to grasp. So I save things like ki for the more advanced students and stick with the simple self-defense techniques for the beginners. Westerners seem to want to learn techniques that are simple and easy to practice."

When Jim Butin is working with students on self-defense in his Oklahoma City dojo, "I don't throw any tournament jive on them," he told me. "They get elbows, knees, knife defense, how to fall, and so on. I reserve all the formal training like the formal stances for a few weeks later. There is such a high turnover rate in any karate class, no matter how slick the instructor is, that I figure why not, for the time they are there, teach them something more practical than the basic stances and blocks and actually give them something that they might be able to use to get out of a tight spot."

"Karate is definitely the most useful art for self-defense for a short time invested," says sociology professor Anson Shupe, an instructor ranked in both judo and isshin-ryu karate. "You can pick up more useful skills quicker in karate than you can in an art like judo," he says. (Now before the judo aficionados get too upset, Dr. Shupe pointed out that judo had several advantages over karate, which we will discuss in chapter six.)

"In judo it takes quite a while just to learn how to fall," Shupe continued. "Take the worst case analysis where I taught a session of just eight lessons at the Y. What are you going to do? Well, I simplified things. You have to be pragmatic. Ideally, you lead them through the progressive stages, but why spend a lot of time stretching, for instance, when they aren't going to continue stretching after they quit?" he asks. "In isshin-ryu we hardly stretch at all anyway because we never kick above the waist."

Hand conditioning is something else Shupe believes is extraneous for a quick course in self-defense.

"That's not going to work real well for women anyway [who take most of the self-defense courses]. I would concentrate on more practical techniques like low kicks and elbows. You have to adapt your teaching methods to the actual situation instead of the ideal one. You've got to be realistic."

Other instructors I spoke to, however, insisted that there was more to learning self-defense than just a knowledge of techniques.

"Self-defense techniques are not the first thing we teach," says John Chung of the Jhoon Rhee Institute. "We want to develop the students' self-confidence first by teaching them what they can do with their bodies. We get them into condition and we teach them how to stretch. When they have that, they feel more secure and they feel like they could actually defend themselves. Self-defense is one of the last things they'll get. If you think you can go out and defend yourself after two months of lessons, that's not true. You can't even get into good shape and develop your self-control in that amount of time."

"I don't know if you need 'self-control' to be able to defend yourself," says long-time instructor Barry Guimbellot. "All you need to do is to be able to hit the other person before he hits you." Guimbellot does agree that it takes time to develop mental and physical discipline, however. "I can remember being a beginner, and the instructors kept saying to relax, relax. Well, it wasn't until I was a brown belt and I had achieved a certain amount of self-confidence that I understood what they meant by being able to mentally relax.

You have to spar for awhile before you can get to that point, though, and we don't let people spar before four to six weeks."

I asked Barry how long, in his experience, the average student stayed with karate. "I'd say half the people drop out anywhere from six weeks to three months into their lessons." That can be a problem if you are trying to work on just mental control and physical conditioning. "That's why I stick to very basic self-defense techniques at first," said Guimbellot. "Then, if anything, they start to think, 'Gee, this is easier than I thought.' That's why I put in at least one fancier technique, maybe a ju-jutsu takedown or something, so they will realize that it does take some work and practice to really get it all down.

"Beginners can't grasp the abstract concepts so I show them very practical self-defense up front. I think that is the way they gain their self-confidence . . . by knowing there is something they could do, even at their stage of development."

Ray McCallum also tries to build the confidence of his students.

"I tell them to analyze the situation. Is it a friend just joking around or is it someone you should be worried about? Try to avoid the situation first, but if you can't avoid it, attack. Be prepared to follow up because sometimes one punch will do it and sometimes it won't. Initiate your attack as soon as possible because when he is attacking you he is the most susceptible to getting hit himself. Again, avoid as long as you can and then go for it."

I asked several instructors, is it realistic to think that a person with just six weeks of karate could defend himself?

"Well, let's just say he's got a definite advantage over the average person," said Guimbellot.

"Six weeks could make them smarter, but only one out of twenty could still react the right way," believes Lori

Lantrip, the number one rated lightweight woman fighter in the country, according to *Karate Illustrated* magazine. She says that the best way to learn how to react properly, especially for women, is "to get out there and fight."

Lantrip is petite; her curly yellow hair frames homecoming queenlike features. You would never suspect how tough she is. I saw her get side kicked in the face during the finals of a large national tournament. She crashed to the mat but just as quickly shrugged off her pain and dizziness to resume the match.

Lori believes in a certain amount of contact in training, but in her Madisonville, Kentucky, school—as in most schools —it takes longer than six months to get to that point.

"You can show people how," says Lori, "but they're not going to be able to do it without really practicing it."

"The average student can't defend himself after only six weeks," flatly states the number four rated fighter in the nation for 1983, Billy Blanks. Like John Chung, Blanks says he reserves most of his serious self-defense training for the students who have proved themselves to be both physically and mentally disciplined. He says that he begins with physical fitness training rather than karate training, something you can believe looking at the size of his arms. "I'm interested in their attitude first," Billy told me. "I find out why they want to study and right out front I test their seriousness. They want to do it all the first day," says this Massachusetts instructor, "but I make them train until it becomes natural."

That is the bottom line. If you want to learn how to defend yourself, you'll have to give karate, or any other martial art, several months before it becomes second nature enough to you so you will be able to use it effectively. By that time I wager you will have seen enough of the other benefits of training that you will want to continue training. No one can guarantee you'll become a black belt, but with enough diligence and discipline, anything is possible!

Karate against a choke

Full-contact karate champion Raymond McCallum is grabbed in a front choke by Steve Selby.

McCallum places his right hand on his opponent's chin and his left hand grabs a handful of hair.

A sharp twist to the left brings the attacker down. Note how McCallum has stepped back and pivoted as his opponent fails.

A punch to the side of the neck finishes the defense.

Karate against a punch

McCallum meets an
incoming punch with a
rising block.

Now he thrusts out a
front kick to the
midsection.

McCallum has grasped
the opponent's right
hand and pulls him
into a straight punch.

Karate against a punch

Here Raymond McCallum stands calmly while being threatened.

As the opponent initiates his punch McCallum shoots out a defensive side kick typical of the direct karate approach.

Since the leg is longer and stronger than the arm it is an effective weapon.

Karate against a punch

Author Keith D. Yates blocks the incoming punch from fellow tae kwon-do stylist Bob Woerner.

He reacts with a quick backfist to the face.

Shifting his weight, Yates does an open-hand strike to the throat.

He finishes with a knee.

Karate against a choke

Keith D. Yates is pinned against a wall by a front choke hold.

A quick slap to the ears stuns the attacker.

Thumbs in the eye sockets further weaken the opponent.

And a knee to the groin finishes him off.

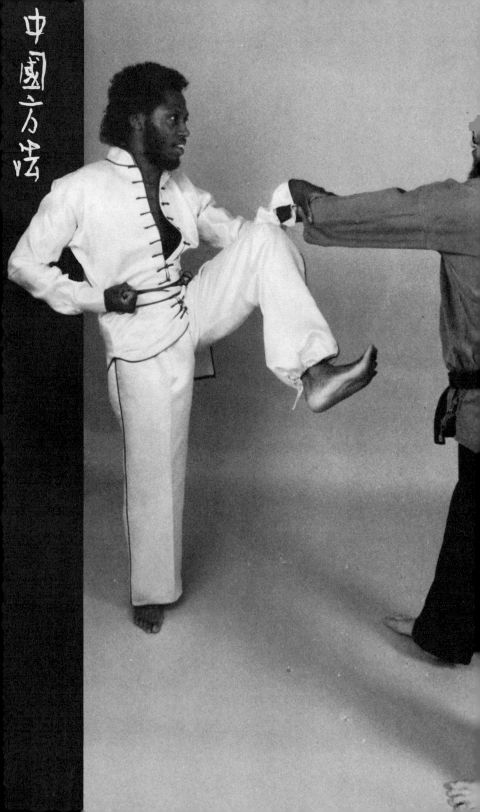

中國方法

CHAPTER FIVE

Kung Fu and Tai Chi

The Chinese Approach

There was a time when many in this country thought of kung fu as merely the Chinese form of karate, but that time has long since passed. Kung fu is actually older than karate and is its own distinct art, or perhaps more accurately, family of arts. Bruce Lee introduced the average American to the Chinese martial arts and Kwai Chang Caine (David Carradine) made kung fu a household word through his television series.

But what is kung fu really? How is it different from karate? How is it the same? I must confess that my own knowledge of Chinese traditions was limited, despite having been in the martial arts for almost twenty years, and so I set out to research and to speak with as many *sifu* ("see-foo" means teacher) as I could to gain a better understanding of and appreciation for the Chinese warrior secrets, and I discovered some fascinating things.

As we have already said, nobody is really certain about the beginnings of the martial arts, although most historians agree that there were fighting methods in China even before Bodhidharma and the Shaolin Temple story (see chapter one). But it is interesting to note that almost all kung fu sifu trace their art back, at least in part, to the Shaolin Temple boxing traditions. In Taiwan, for example, all the hard Chinese styles are specifically called *Shaolin.*

Incidentally, the term kung fu功夫(which is Mandarin; in Cantonese it is gung fu) has been erroneously adopted as referring to the Chinese martial arts in the West.

According to Sam Chin, a tai chi chuan instructor I spoke to, "Gung fu just means the work and time put into something. In Chinese society, like in Chinatowns, especially in New York or San Francisco, they might say to a good cook or chef in a restaurant, 'Oh, you have good gung fu'; that just means this person is well trained.

"*Wushu* is the official name in China for the martial arts. *Wu* means fighting or military and *shu* means art," says Chin, a native of China. In the 1950s wushu was standardized and is now in the public curriculum in mainland China. It is officially stressed as a sport (they hold regular wushu competitions) rather than as a military fighting art.

As I read through stories about the Shaolin Temple (actually there were several different temple-like monasteries that later came to be known as Shaolin) I kept coming across different versions. One said there was a division between the fighting monks and the non-fighting monks. Another said that the only fighting monks were actually bandits who had so disguised themselves. I suppose we can only say that evidence seems to suggest that in more than one monastery the fighting arts were used as tools for spiritual advancement.

Remember, however, that China is an immense country which has had a vast population for millennia. Large groups of people developed independently from one another. Therefore to say that all Chinese warrior arts can be directly connected to *one* single tradition is highly speculative. Let's just say that as the Shaolin influence spread, it no doubt influenced many of the developing schools. It took quite some time for what we might call modern systems to evolve.

There are indications that the first organized style was the *chang chuan* (long fist) system said to have been created around 970 A.D. It is a wide-open style; that is to say, it contains a great variety of hand and foot techniques.

Kung fu systems in rural north China tended to be very mixed because as teachers with varying degrees of ability and emphasis traveled from village to village many versions of chang chuan arose. Although the basic system is very generalized, it can be noted for its wide sweeping fist techniques and low stances with high kicks, characteristic of the northern style.

Brian Duffy, a rated kata competitor and Chinese stylist, outlined for me some of the differences between northern and southern styles.

"The northern country is more open farmland so the movements are characterized by long-sweeping, long-range type movements, because if you were attacked in a field you had more room to move around in.

"The southern part of the country is more urbanized," says Duffy. "Very close little alleys and shops, and so those systems are characterized by stronger low stances and rapid hand movements and not so much the acrobatic movements (of the northern schools)."

"Northern styles," adds Eric Lee, one of the most famous kung fu competitors and instructors in the country, "are usually taken more by people with longer legs and more reach because they place more emphasis on the legs. In the northern areas of China there is more grassy, open area where in the south it is more rocky and you don't want to jump too much," says Lee. "And a lot of southern style kung fu people live on boats and that eliminates certain high kicks."

The northern stylists spend a great amount of time on stretching techniques so that they can jump and kick. Perhaps the most spectacular of all, and the favorite of the kung fu movies, is the flying side kick. You'll see this technique in karate and tae kwon-do as well, but however impressive it looks in the pictures it really isn't too practical because you have to take at least a couple of steps to be able to jump high enough to kick someone in the face. It is believed that this kick was originally designed to knock a mounted cavalry-man off his horse, however, and in that role it probably was highly effective.

The southern schools tend to depreciate the jumping kicks, putting more emphasis on solid and steady stances. The river people of the south, with their strong oarsman's torsos and arms, developed deflecting blows and simultaneous hand strikes. The typical southern stylist will never allow an arm to be grabbed but will continually move his limbs in deflections, slaps, punches, and an occasional foot sweep or groin kick. Wooden dummies with protruding arms are used frequently by southern stylists. Repeated strikes to the dummy not only perfects technique but conditions the forearms and hands. I must point out here, as in the discussion on different styles of karate, that these are mere generalizations. Most teachers, especially in this country, will mix hand and foot blows as well as hard and soft techniques.

I asked Dan Inosanto, one of Bruce Lee's first students, about the relative strengths of each of the different approaches.

"That's kind of like asking if a graduate of East Texas State is really as good as a graduate of the University of Houston. It's really an individual thing. Southerners are supposed to be good with their hands and northerners are supposed to be good with their feet, but I've seen southern guys who could kick like northerners, and so you really can't put a label on it."

Brian Duffy is a regular winner in forms and weapons competitions who hails from Austin, Texas, where he teaches Chinese *kenpo.* He also does *hung gar,* a southern style. Hung gar is a popular system which emphasizes very low stances and isometric breathing exercises. It contains many weapons as well—typical of some of the Chinese styles.

"Chinese systems do tend to have a wide variety of weapons," Brian told me. "The Japanese system is pretty standardized with the bo, the sword, the kama, and a few others. But the Chinese have a tremendously wide variety of weapons, and I have personally become very entertained with it."

Weapons training is one of the reasons Robert Hartfield, a black belt in tae kwon-do, switched to kung fu.

"Kung fu uses more weapons than any other system of martial art that I've done," says Robert. You can see Chinese practitioners using swords, spears, staffs, even fans (with metal ribs). Harfield particularly likes the three-sectional staff which has helped him to achieve the status of a nationally ranked weapons competitor.

Another thing you'll see in kung fu but not karate are shoes. This distinction is also traced back to geographical reasons. Because of the rocky and uneven land in some parts of China the people always wore shoes, even when practicing their martial art. On Okinawa, where, as we know, karate originated, the terrain was more soft sand and so many of the natives went without shoes.

Another tradition that the Chinese arts especially embrace is herbal medicine. Again, the practice can be traced back to ancient times when many masters realized that a fighter was only as strong as his own body. Emphasis was placed on ointments, baths, and herbal preparations.

"Most kung fu masters are herbalists and acupuncturists," says Hartfield. "They understand how the body functions and how its energy is channeled. For instance, most Chinese are able to do breaking techniques without any callouses because they use specialized herbal medicine. Their hands will still have a smooth texture and yet they have the same proficiency and the same effect as the karate masters who have the gigantic callouses."

I asked Duffy to explain his style of Chinese kenpo, which is usually considered a style of karate. "It's a cross between the straight-line linear movements of Japanese karate and the soft circular movements of Chinese kung fu," said Duffy. "It's called a hard/soft system. It has elements of both in it.

"I'm a member of the National Chinese Kenpo Karate Association. In Kenpo you have Japanese Kenpo, Chinese Kenpo, American Kenpo, and Okinawan Kenpo, depending on what you emphasize. We emphasize the Chinese aspects of the art," said Duffy.

So is it a Chinese or a Japanese art? Brian says that it is kind of a cross. "Kenpo is the Japanese translation of the

Fig. 18 The five animals of kung fu. The Shaolin systems are said to have been founded, at least in part, on the five animals. They represent the ideal combination of hard and soft movements, internal and external energy. They are the dragon, the snake, the tiger, the leopard, and the crane.

word *ch'uan fa,* meaning the way of the fist, that was taught in the Shaolin temple."

How can the average person tell the difference between kung fu, Chinese and Japanese kenpo, or even Japanese karate?

"It depends on which aspect you're looking at," replied Duffy. "If you go to a tournament and you watch people fight, there's not a lot of difference in styles because everybody's doing 'sport karate.' You just go out and do the techniques that are going to score points for you. Judging forms is where you can see a lot of difference in the fact that Japanese, Korean, and even Okinawan styles are very power-oriented systems. The Japanese and Korean styles tend to be very straight-line, linear in motion. In Korea, especially, there is an emphasis on power in a single strike, whereas the Chinese systems tend to be characterized by more flowing circular movements. That's why they are called softer styles. They are not soft because you hit any softer," he hastened to add. "But their movements are just more circular, more rounded off."

Tae kwon-do may be "better for kicks," agrees number one rated woman's form competitor, Cynthia Rothrock, but Chinese styles are "more expressive and graceful," she believes. That's why she sticks with kung fu forms in tournaments, although she teaches both kung fu and tae kwon-do. Disturbed by the unequal emphasis in the past on fighting, the new generation of forms competitors, like Cyndi, are forcing people to take note of the more traditional aspects of the martial arts with their inspiring performances.

"As forms competitors are becoming more progressive and innovative, so are the fighters," she told me. Rothrock practices a northern style of kung fu known as *eagle claw,* which she classifies as a "strong style." Her flashy Chinese movements not only have positioned her at the very top of the women's division, but she is rated number one in the overall weapons division as well by *Karate Illustrated* magazine. *Black Belt* magazine named her the 1983 "Female Competitor of the Year."

"Karate emphasizes more strength and clarity. There are more straight-line blocks and other techniques," said Rothrock. "Kung fu is more circular with faster combinations of hand techniques, although nowadays you see more combinations of both approaches, especially in competition."

She declined to say which art would have an advantage in a confrontation, saying, "It depends totally on the individual. You could have someone who is outstanding in tae kwon-do, for example, and someone who is only moderately good in kung fu, or vice-versa, and it's too hard to say. It depends on the individual.

"Kung fu is more graceful and more beautiful, however. It's not just fast and flowing with no power though, like some people think. It's just that the timing changes the look. As far as the way I am built and how I feel when I'm performing, I like to do kung fu."

Arlene Limas is the top rated woman's fighting competitor in the country at just eighteen years old. She has studied kung fu for thirteen years.

"Kung fu is good for someone who can't fight force against force, which is mostly what an art like karate bases itself on. If you do a karate cross block, for example, it's force against force. In a soft style it's all deflecting and circular. You never meet anything head-on and this makes it good for people who are small and don't have the weight to go force against force."

A recent article in *Inside Kung-Fu* magazine admitted that all things being equal, the forceful power of a karate fighter versus the finesse of a kung fu fighter would probably result in a victory for the direct and simple approach, i.e., karate. Paradoxically this weakness against an equally trained karateka turns out to be a strength against the street fighter. That is to say, the complexity of the Chinese approach gives the kung fu stylist a versatility and flexibility that some karate fighters lack. Most karate people are trained on the "one strike" principle, that is, a maximum attack in the shortest amount of time. Kung fu is more concerned with mastering the subtle deflections and body moves to throw off the attacker and thus be able to strike in the most efficient manner possible.

Now we have spoken of the northern/southern division of kung fu but there is another dividing line we can draw. That is the distinction between *internal* and *external* styles. This is also a difficult area to be dogmatic about because in many cases it's hard to tell where external practice leaves off and internal training begins. To be sure, all martial arts rely on both physical and mental discipline (as we discussed in chapter three) but, in the Chinese system especially, you can see this internal aspect.

"It has to do with the way power is derived," says Duffy, speaking of this division. "External power is musculature power which comes from various training methods such as calisthenics, isometrics, things like that. Internal systems get their power from ch'i, the life-force."

Eric Lee agrees, saying, "Internal styles are more into internal breathing and meditation and methods that develop that internal strength."

Jane Hallandar is a kung fu practitioner from San Francisco and a noted author on the Chinese arts. She told me that "although we do see some internal studies done in Korean martial arts and even in Indonesian arts, the Chinese seem to have gone into a greater detail (because) they have a longer history. Basically," according to Hallandar, "the difference (between internal and external) is that the external training conditions the bone, muscles, and extremities of the body, while internal training develops the ch'i, the internal energy of the body, and the internal organs, and so it promotes longevity and better health, and it actually achieves far superior strength in the martial arts."

John Painter, a *tao ch'i chuan* instructor, says that while "most external martial arts, like Shaolin, have concepts of ch'i, it is really more *tung chin,* which means body force properly applied." He explains that when you are doing your forms (or sets as they are called in kung fu) you try to align your body properly and concentrate on correct technique and power. Then "your body parts are working like a machine, like a unit. When that happens," says Painter, "you are producing what would be called in Japan, *ki,* but what is called in China tung chin. You are producing just physical body force. But in your internal martial arts, which include *pa-kua, hsing-i, tai chi chuan,* and *aikido* in Japan—these arts are based solely, completely, and wholly on ch'i, a deeper internal power."

In spite of these distinctions in approach, it would not be

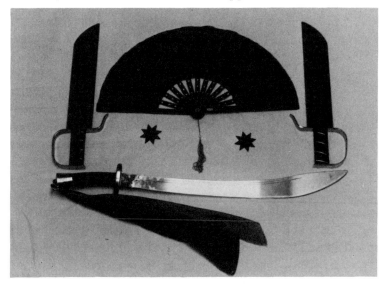

Fig. 19 Kung fu makes use of many weapons. Shown here are *butterfly swords,* a *Chinese fan,* throwing stars or *shuriken,* and the *kung fu sword.*

too far off to say that in their very advanced forms the Chinese arts *all* tend to become the same, a mixture of hard and soft, external and internal. Jane Hallandar points out that "some systems start out with external training and work to the internal, and others go the other way around." Hallandar, who has been to Hong Kong several times, as well as to China, says, "My experience has been that most masters in Hong Kong who have a great background [in various arts] seem to prefer to start the student in an external style until he gets a good foundation in the basics, and then go into internal training, like tai chi, and that in turn will develop their external kung fu."

I asked Jane to compare the kung fu in Hong Kong to that in the United States.

"I live in San Francisco and so the kung fu you see here is going to be a lot different than the kung fu you see around the country," she said. "In San Francisco there is no room for the diluted version because there is so much competition from the Chinese. A lot of people are teaching a Westernized version though. They've mixed it up with karate or something like that."

Indeed, the Chinese styles, like the Japanese, Okinawan, and Korean arts, are changing as they become more popular in this country. Some instructors who prefer a more traditional approach bemoan what a USC kung fu sifu says is the "assembly line approach." A lot of schools run by Westerners did rush out to paint "kung fu" on their windows when the TV show became popular. Many of the Chinese teachers were still reluctant, however, to teach non-Chinese, and American teachers were often not at a sufficiently advanced level to teach anything more than the dancelike sets devoid of the power and application to be found at those higher levels. Perhaps this is how kung fu got the reputation for containing only soft graceful movements without any practical self-defense value.

Today there are many competent American sifu as well as a large number of Chinese instructors who have come to this country. Like all martial arts that have come to the United States, kung fu has evolved to fit the American mindset.

"It's turned 180 degrees," says Dan Inosanto. "And Americans will take it to a higher level because of their thinking." Inosanto believes that Americans don't have the religious and political prejudices that have prevented the Asians from sharing their techniques and so they are more open to learning from one another.

One of the things you see often here that is not found in the traditional approach is belt rankings.

"In traditional kung fu there is no belt system and no sash system," Jane Hallandar told me. "Some instructors have modernized it and instituted a sash system which is sort of the reverse of karate, but traditionally there are no belts or sashes at all."

Arlene Limas, also known as "Lady Kung Fu," a Shaolin stylist, explains further. "I was taught where there were only two belts, a black sash and a white sash, but that's the opposite of what we have here now. We go from white to black," (Arlene's school in Chicago has other belt colors as well) "but I learned that you went from black sash, where you are supposedly in the dark, to white sash, where you are enlightened and open and can see everything clearly."

Robert Hartfield has colored belts leading to black belt in his Dallas kung fu school as well.

"Americans, being the way they are, like to see proof of their progression," he explains, "and they want to get that coveted black belt. And so we teach an Americanized version in that sense, although I do stress the traditional values in that I tell my students that the knowledge is more important than the belt. A belt can be taken away but your knowledge can't be."

When you speak with kung fu stylists who are on the tournament circuit, and winning, they admit that they have adapted techniques from many different systems. Hartfield, as we said, was already a black belt in tae kwon-do when he started his kung fu training and says he still does a lot of hard Korean-style kicks when he competes. Arlene Limas studied Okinawan shorin-ryu for a while with past champion Keith Vitali to augment her years of Chinese training. I asked Arlene if her fighting approach was a compilation of different styles.

"Sure, it's pretty much Americanized in that respect. If you ever see me or any of my students doing forms [however], it's soft-style moves, like the *praying mantis* style, although we do it like you were fighting on the street; in other words, done very hard. My instructor was a soft-style teacher but he always taught it hard."

Some stylists, indeed, pride themselves on their eclectic approach. Eric Lee is one of the best known proponents of *won hop kuen do,* the style devised by Al Decascas.

"We keep some traditional forms and weapons but we also compete in the creative division where you are free to choreograph your own movements." (Eric earned his nickname, "The Little King of Kata," for his electrifying original forms performances.)

"As far as actual techniques go," says Lee, "we have no restrictions there either. We can do anything we want. If someone is coming at me I can punch him before he touches me or I can duck and slip a punch into his groin, or I can turn and give him a back kick or can use a sound effect, like yelling *STOP,* and then punch him when he freezes for a second. It is totally up to the individual. All our students have their own style. We have no set defenses and so are totally unorthodox."

If that sounds undisciplined, it really isn't. But several people have told me that kung fu classes do tend to be a little less formal than other styles.

Fig. 20 Eric Lee started his kung fu training as a teenager in San Francisco in the wing chun style. He soon began studying Al Dacascos' won hop kuen do, which is more of an eclectic system. Lee's spectacular Chinese forms demonstrations earned him the name "Little King of Kata." For four years straight (1970-1974) he was the number one rated weapons and forms competitor, winning over 200 trophies. Eric has acquired proficiency in the use of over twenty different weapons. Besides writing a book on the subject of self-defense he has appeared in numerous television shows and movies.

Lee encourages new students to stick with their training. "Even though only 20 percent of the people are going to be really good, everyone should try their best. I constantly try to motivate my students," says Lee. "I tell them to give it more time—in six months they will be a lot better. Of course, you can't expect to get better just by sitting there—you have to train. If your mind is analytical and you are perceptive and disciplined, you can really go far."

"In my experience, the karate training was more disciplined," says George Chung, the nation's top forms competitor, who has studied both tae kwon-do and kung fu. "There was more 'yes sir, no sir.' The Chinese systems seemed more casual in their training."

Chung explains why. "It is very difficult to teach large masses kung fu because it is so intricate. You have to get around to the students more, and so a lot of the kung fu training is one-on-one, or one to just two or three. You need more individualized instruction.

"In a karate form you might have 20 moves, while in a Chinese form you might have 70, 80, even 100. Of course it depends on the individual instructor, but I've found that in a karate class the actual training is more difficult physically, but the teaching (or learning) is more difficult in kung fu."

"That's true," agrees Limas. "It is a very personalized process to teach kung fu. In a karate class you can teach everyone a down block, for example, [at the same time] and it's pretty easy; but in kung fu, because it's more circular, you have to move the body more."

"Kung fu stresses more individual perfection," Robert Hartfield told me. "The movements are more intricate and more complicated. It just requires a lot more attention to posture and balance and coordination."

"There are more facets to kung fu than a lot of Japanese systems," states Hallandar, "because a lot of the Japanese or Korean systems don't have the number of weapons or two-man sets available or mechanical training devices (like the wooden dummy), and in that respect it takes longer. But as far as mastering the basics, and that's what self-defense is, I think that it's going to take any student a reasonable amount of time in *any* of the martial arts."

What about kung fu for self-defense? Does the intricacy of the Chinese approach make it less suitable for a quick self-defense program? Arlene Limas, for one, says yes.

"If you have a person who is coming in for a three-month course and she just wants to learn how to protect herself, kung fu's going to be rough. Traditional kung fu is for the more dedicated student," says Limas. "I have different classes. I have a competition class, and an exercise class, and a women's self-defense class, and I teach them all a little bit differently."

George Chung also modifies his self-defense training. "There's no sense in taking them through the whole rigamarole. I'm not degrading the art by just teaching the person self-defense if all he wants to learn is self-defense. As an instructor I have the prerogative to say 'yes' or 'no,' and if that's all a person wants, I'll say 'yes.' Now, I will use a little more of the Chinese approach perhaps in that I'll break down each technique for them and work with them a little closer."

What marks the Chinese approach to self-defense, I wondered.

"Well, the Chinese systems were developed where the ancient masters used to watch the animals," says Brian Duffy. "So we have a lot of clawing and ripping and gouging to facial areas. There are strikes to nerve centers of the body as well as to the throat and groin and lymph node areas.

"There was a system called *demak* which is called the death touch," says Duffy, "which worked off striking the various acupressure points at various times of the day and also the lymph nodes. In old China the diet used to be so bad that the lymph nodes were the areas of the body that retained the poisons. They would draw the poisons out of the food they ate, keeping it out of their systems. By striking the lymph node areas," claims Duffy, "and bursting them to release those poisons into their body, the person would get sick and die after a period of time. It also had to do with transference of chi or internal energy into the body, but when you look at it and analyze it, it had a lot to do with the diet."

"Some say the Chinese approach to self-defense is more defensive," says Eric Lee, "but [it is] more offensive because in a real situation it doesn't matter what style you are, the rule is, hit first, hit hard, and hit fast. But as far as the Chinese style of self-defense goes, every teacher has different techniques or specialties in their own areas. They are all good but sometimes you have to make them better. Some have to be modified to make them more effective for modern days. Some, however, are good as they are," says Lee.

John Painter makes a good point when he acknowledges, "as far as self-defense goes, any martial art is very limited because, according to statistics, every seventh car that passes has some form of lethal weapon in it and most are firearms. You also have to realize that in most real situations [at least those not involving guns] you only need four or five techniques, and that's all, so [one might ask] what's all that other stuff for?

"To me," Painter continues, "a real martial art, and I guess I don't really like the word martial very much, is one that makes a whole, integrated human being."

The late Bruce Lee once said, "Before I studied the art, a punch to me was just a punch, a kick just a kick. After I learned the art, a punch is no longer a punch, a kick no longer a kick. Now that I've understood the art, a punch is just a punch, a kick just a kick."

Indeed, of all the martial arts, the Chinese seem most to realize that physical techniques alone do not make an art. Of all the styles that come out of China, none delve so deeply into this philosophy as the so-called internal arts.

But before we examine, albeit briefly, the three main internal systems, let's run down the names and attributes of some more of the Shaolin external styles. I realize I am risking the wrath of some practitioners whose systems I will leave out, but my purposes here are only to familiarize you with some of the names. The comments will have to be brief

Fig. 21 The *yin and yang* circle symbolizes the balance of the positive and negative forces of the universe. The wavy line in the middle represents the constant
flow between the elements and the little dots show that even within the yin there
is yang and vice versa. The eight outside trigrams are from the *I-Ching* or *Book
of Changes*. The yin/yang circle is the symbol of tai chi, while the art of pa-kua
(which means "eight diagrams") is based on the I-Ching.

and pretty general, because, as we have seen, there are variations within variations that permeate any so-called style or system.

We've already mentioned that *chang chuan* is perhaps the oldest northern Shaolin style. Another old northern system is northern *praying mantis,* which, according to tradition, was founded by a kung fu master named Wong Long toward the end of the Ming Dynasty. He studied the fighting technique of the praying mantis insect and developed the mantis claw, the trademark grabbing motion of the style which is used to poke, grip, or apply pressure to an opponent's joints. That original system is known as "seven-star praying mantis" although today you can find several variations such as "eight steps" which place more emphasis on in-close fighting; "six-harmony," developed to concentrate on more internal power; and "tai chi praying mantis," which, despite its name, is not related to tai chi chuan.

Many kung fu styles were patterned after animals, and so we have *monkey style,* known for its tumbling, rolling and jumping techniques; and *eagle claw,* which resembles some forms of Japanese *ju-jutsu* with its joint locks and fast takedowns.

The five original forms of southern kung fu were created strictly as fighting arts during the violent area of the Ching Dynasty. Therefore, unlike some of the older northern styles which were practiced during more peaceful times, they taught quick external methods of combat first, followed by internal training.

The only original southern style seen today is the popular hung gar, which we have already mentioned. Known for its wide, low stances and many isometric breathing exercises, it seems to be a little slower than some of the other kung fu systems. Although it appears to be an external style, it makes much use of internal training at advanced levels, and traditional hung gar schools all post the moralistic philosophy of its founder, Wong Fei Hung, on their walls.

It is estimated that over 30 percent of the martial arts practitioners in Hong Kong do *choy-li-fut*. Founded in 1836, it is a favorite of many full-contact fighters in Southeast Asia because of its famous long-armed power, where the arm becomes like a rope and the fist like a dart attached to its end. Choy-li-fut also contains many weapons in its training, with the most popular being the staff and the butterfly knives (fig. 19).

One of the more well-known styles of kung fu in this country is win chun, the original style of Bruce Lee. Tradition has it that the founder was a woman, Yim Wing Chun. Her system was much more simple and direct than the other Shaolin styles. Blocks are used merely to redirect an incoming blow so as to counter with a short punch (the one-inch type made famous by Lee). Another well-known and unique feature of win chun practice is sticky hands or *chi sao*. Here, two stylists face each other, moving their forearms in small circles, maintaining constant wrist contact to train their sensitivity and ability to predict an opponent's movements.

We could go on for several pages on other variations of both northern and southern Shaolin styles, but unless you are a kung fu connoisseur, which I am not, the names and techniques all start to become confusing after a while. Suffice it to say there are enough variations so that you ought to be able to find something you like.

As Eric Lee says, "To each his own. The reason people take different styles is because there are many different personalities."

One of the most famous personalities out of China's past is Lao Tzu, who wrote the canon of Taoist philosophy around 300 B.C. Basically Taoism teaches that by constantly observing the present state of things one can discover true harmony. Through meditation, Taoists seek to experience man's natural place in the world. These are the goals of China's internal martial arts, *hsing-i, pa-kua,* and *tai chi chuan.*

Hsing-i, which literally means "shape of mind," is a very old system originating about 1640 A.D. There are several kinds of hsing-i, from a more external, straight-forward style *(hopei),* which doesn't go as deeply into the internal aspects, to a highly sophisticated system wherein the techniques are more akin to animal movements than to fight sequences. At the most advanced levels the master is said to be able to emit power (ch'i) without any physical effort.

Hsing-i is frequently taught in conjunction with pa-kua. Supposedly the great hsing-i teacher, Kuo Yun-Shen, challenged Tung Hai-ch'uan, the first pa-kua master, sometime toward the end of the eighteenth century. They battled for three days until the pa-kua master finally won, whereupon the two swore to teach their arts jointly.

Pa-kua means "eight diagrams," which refers to the eight trigrams or eight changes of the ancient Confucian text, the I-Ching (see fig. 21). The pa-kua practitioner circles constantly, focusing on subtle evasive action based largely on the I-Ching philosophy of change. The Taoist belief in the eternally changing nature of the world dictates that the student become one with the process of change and "go with the flow," so to speak.

We now come to the third main internal system, the oft misunderstood *tai chi chuan* 太極拳 (grand ultimate fist).

Although the beginnings of tai chi chuan are obscure (aren't they all?), one legend has it that a Taoist priest, Jang San Feng, was sitting meditating next to his window when he noticed a commotion outside. A bird and a snake were engaged in a life-and-death struggle. Jang observed how the animals could be both relaxed and quick at the same time.

From this initial observation, it is said, tai chi originated. However it began, tai chi chuan has become the most practiced martial art in the world, with millions practicing it daily in the streets of every great city of China as well as Hong Kong, Singapore, and in the Chinese quarters of American cities. Westerners have taken to this ancient art as well, but most view it as a slow-motion, yogalike exercise. Even some teachers of other styles of the Chinese arts whom I spoke with relegated tai chi to the role of a "healing art for health and equilibrium" only.

Jane Hallandar believes that is partly because most people are not exposed to the final, advanced stage of tai chi, which contains hard and fast power along with the soft flowing movements. She says that "it has been diluted not only in the United States but even in places like Hong Kong and China."

Jeff Wager, a tai chi instructor from Master Waysun Liao's Tao Center in Chicago, agrees wholeheartedly. According to Jeff, the original classical style was watered down by a man named Yang Lu Chan in the late nineteenth century.

"The emperor had held his family hostage because he wanted him (Yang Lu Chan) to teach him personally," Jeff told me. "In order to get his family released, Yang Lu Chan gave the impression he was teaching the authentic art and got his family released, but in fact he only gave them the outer shell without all the internal workings and the internal power development."

Most of the tai chi styles being taught today are descendants of that watered down version, Wager claims. Their school, of course, is one of the few still teaching the original system.

Whether or not the story is completely true, it certainly *can* be stated that today's most popular styles *(chen, yang, sun,* and two separate schools that are both translated as

wu) are taught in such a manner that all people, the young
and the very old, can practice and benefit from their slow
circular exercises.

How different are the various styles? I asked Sam Chin, a
Dallas sifu.

"Let me give you an easy example," he replied. "It's
like the Methodists and the Baptists. Basically they have the
same source, but people might practice it with some minor
differences. So many people are changing the forms today
that it is difficult to divide it up so neatly."

In mainland China the State Physical Culture and Sports
Commission in 1956 introduced a simplified version of tai
chi for the masses. Sixty percent of the postures were dropped
or combined with other moves to greatly reduce the time to
learn the basics of the art. Some traditional instructors naturally were not too crazy about the changes, but classical
tai chi has not died out in China as they feared, as many still
do the more advanced versions as a panacea for everything
from liver trouble to neurotic anxiety.

"Many people who do it were once weak and sickly,"
explains Chin. "If you play something very rapidly and move
fast like some of the external-type exercises, you might actually be hurting the person's body. You see, the slow-motion
movements gradually bring up internal strength. You have
the balance, the coordination, and gradually the muscles and
the blood circulation are improved."

I have to admit my own prejudice as a hard style martial
artist that, while tai chi forms do look like good exercise,
they still do not *look* like effective self-defense. Indeed many
Westerners never get beyond the obvious health and spiritual
benefits to the practical fighting aspects that the masters
claim tai chi clearly has.

"I see in the magazines where they say tai chi is just exercise for women or old people," Chin exclaims. "That is ridicu-
lous. Tai chi is mainly a martial art. We train people slowly,

to improve their balance and coordination so that when they know what they are doing they can respond very fast. When you come to self-defense you don't do slow any more, you have to be fast."

"The slow-motion stuff is only part of it," agrees Wager. "There's blinding speed in tai chi too. People aren't aware of that. They don't understand that it's all in the way you use your ch'i. But," he continues, "tai chi is mainly spiritual development."

The tai chi chuan symbol is the familiar yin and yang circle (fig. 21). It pictures the Taoist belief that life contains a blending of positive and negative forces continuously flowing into one another. Tai chi is perhaps the pinnacle of martial practice combined with Taoist philosophy. Yin and yang imply that strength lies in softness and in yielding. In practice this means that deflecting and counterattacking will defeat an opponent who relies upon strength alone. This whole concept of flowing demands slowness and relaxation, which are said to promote inner calmness.

The principle exercise, other than the slow motion forms, is called "push-hands" or *toy sao*. Two people lift their hands making contact at the wrists. One person pushes while the other curves the attack off to the side. The power is to come from the waist while the body remains relaxed. The elbows are down and the shoulders are dropped. Chin says push-hands can be done together as a family, and indeed it frequently becomes quite a social activity. It has been said that the push-hands exercise enables you to know and understand the other person. Eventually you get to the point where you can feel your opponent's next move rather than see it.

Tai chi chuan is a fascinating system, but all agree that it takes many, many years to master.

"It takes half a lifetime for the roots to take hold and grow," says Wager. "You will never exhaust this art, and the abilities you can achieve in it are endless as long as you keep on practicing, because ultimately it's not dependent on the physical, and that's what makes it different."

Kung fu against a choke

Kung fu champion Eric Lee is about to be grabbed by top forms competitor Robert Hartfield.

Before the choke can be applied, Lee strikes out with a spear hand to the throat. Notice how he has shifted his weight slightly forward for maximum reach and power.

Lee now shifts his weight back to his rear leg . . .

and finishes off with a side thrust kick.

Kung fu against a punch

Here Lee and Hartfield square off.

As Hartfield begins a punching attack, Lee drops to one side, a typical kung fu evasive maneuver.

Now he shoots out an open back hand strike to the groin.

Shifting his weight back . . .

Lee breaks his opponent's knee with a side kick kick.

CHAPTER SIX

Ju·jutsu, Judo, and Aikido

The Empty-Handed Arts of Japan

I had been teaching tae kwon-do for a number of years when a friend invited me to participate in an informal workout with a ju-jutsu instructor who had recently moved into town. We all enjoyed it so much we decided to continue meeting on a weekly basis. We got together every Wednesday from 9 P.M. to usually past midnight (those were my single days). There were just five of us in the class. Four were black belts in tae kwon-do and the other fellow was already a black belt in ju-jutsu who wanted some additional training in another style.

It was a different type of training than we were used to. In tae kwon-do we covered throws and falls only briefly, but here we started every class with forward falls, side falls, and back falls. We worked on stretching the wrists rather than the legs and we got used to tapping the mat to indicate we were in pain from a joint hold-down.

The instructor was a tall, muscular man named Ted Gambordella. Ted is not only a martial arts expert (he holds black belts in several arts), but a recognized authority on physical fitness. He's written a number of books on exercising, sports injuries, karate, and ju-jutsu.

"Ju-jutsu is a confused and fragmented art today," he says. "In real ju-jutsu, the way it was in the days of the samurai, you had throws, wrist locks, punches, kicks, even weapons. In my style, for example, you had to know 280 different techniques to get a black belt. In karate you may only have to know 30. We had to know the karate kicks, punches, and blocks, *plus* all the throws, chokes, wrist locks, finger locks, and pressure points. So it's a very broad art."

Ju-jutsu is closely related to the arts of judo and aikido, being, in fact, their parent art. None of these three is as widely found or taught in this country as the other arts we have covered so far in this book. The average person may not even have heard of them, or at least has no idea of what they are all about. The serious martial art student, however,

Fig. 22 Drawing from an old Japanese print showing ju-jutsu joint locking techniques.

should have at least some understanding of their purposes and approaches.

Most scholars say that the first ju-jutsu system was founded in 1532 by Takenouchi Hisamori. The late martial arts historian, Donn Draeger, said that there were empty-handed ju-jutsu techniques in Japan long before that, of course, but that Takenouchi's system provided the first base upon which other systems could be built. And build they did. There are 725 officially documented styles of Japanese ju-jutsu. Many, if not most, of them are no longer practiced.

Ju-jutsu was and is a generic term that can be applied to numerous and varied systems of ancient unarmed combat. Actually, it was not a major offensive tactic for the ancient Japanese bushi (warriors), for they relied mainly on their swords. Ju-jutsu's greatest period was from the late seventeenth century to the mid-nineteenth century. With the advent of peaceful times and with the conversion of many warriors from bujutsu to budo (see chapter one for a more detailed explanation), ju-jutsu began to lose its combativeness and its popularity. That, combined with the fact that rival ju-jutsu schools frequently engaged in death matches where innocent persons sometimes became victims, led to ju-jutsu becoming synonymous with unsavory elements in the minds of the general public.

In 1905, most of the old ju-jutsu schools merged with the Kodokan (judo) although the aiki-jutsu schools decided to remain independent. In the United States there are no governing organizations, and several ju-jutsu experts I have spoken with consider this a real weakness.

As I've said, both judo and aikido came from ju-jutsu. According to some, these two systems are better termed sports rather than self-defense combat arts, and we'll explore them both a little later in this chapter.

Ju-jutsu Today

Ju-jutsu (sometimes spelled jujitsu in the West) means the art of flexibility or gentleness. As mentioned, there are a number of different styles or schools, each with its own emphasis.

"Some emphasize striking techniques, or *atemi waza*," says Dallas instructor, Steve Weiss (the ju-jutsu black belt who was in the class with me). "Others specialize in throwing, some in joint-locking techniques."

Steve had trained in several different types of ju-jutsu from several different instructors. I asked him how the various approaches differed.

"Well, I've seen a lot that vary in their strategy and principles and applications as well as just their techniques. I've seen some styles that do nothing but joint-locks, I've seen some that do nothing but striking and choking. But most of them do a little bit of all but specialize in one thing, usually throwing."

Los Angeles instructor George Kirby is of the opinion that there are really no styles, only the art of ju-jutsu.

"Despite the many approaches," he told me, "by the time you get to shodan (first degree black belt) they are all very similar, and you end up knowing pretty much the same things." But when I asked about the division of hard styles and soft styles, he answered, "Oh, there is a whole spectrum, yes. Some are more karatelike, some more like judo, some like hapkido. But as I've said they all tend to merge and blend until they are very similar by the time you get to black belt. I sometimes describe ju-jutsu as a combination of judo, karate, and aikido because people can understand and relate to that better. Of course, judo, aikido, and even some styles of karate really come from ju-jutsu." In his book on ju-jutsu, Kirby even suggests dividing ju-jutsu instruction into these three broad areas, judo for throws and leverage, karate for strikes and hits, and aikido for the use of attacker momentum.

Ju-jutsu is like karate in yet another way. Because of the many styles and instructors it is as organizationally fragmented as American karate. Kirby has tried to organize the art with the American Jujutsu Association, of which he is the president, and with his association with the AAU, but he admits it is an almost impossible task.

"There really aren't many qualified teachers in this country," says Kirby. "Most instructors seem to prefer to teach through YMCAs or city parks rather than at a private dojo (thus remaining independent)."

"Anyone can become a ju-jutsu master today," warns long-time instructor, Darryl Craig. "In judo there is always someone above you saying you have to know this and this, but that's not true in ju-jutsu, at least not in this country. As a result we have a lot of people running around saying they are ju-jutsu teachers but they are not. They are usually only half-assed karate people."

Craig has traveled to Japan from his Houston home "too many times to count" and has studied with some of the great masters there. He holds black belts not only in ju-jutsu, but in karate, judo, and kobudo as well. His style is *kasho gushin budo ju-jutsu* which, according to Craig, is "police self-defense techniques."

"Ju-jutsu is a very nasty word in Japan and so they call it *taiho jutsu,* meaning body arts," says Craig. "My style is a kodokan-approved taiho jutsu, which teaches techniques like how to move people along when they don't want to move and how to arrest them."

Since master Craig knows so many different approaches, I wondered which art he advises for new students in his dojo.

"I don't start them out in *any* art. I let them make their choice. I have them watch a complete class before I even talk to them. It's not for me to decide because it's their destiny.

Fig. 23 Dennis Palumbo began his formal studies of the martial arts in 1959 with the *yangi daito ryu* style of aiki-jutsu in Lynwood, California. He was stationed in Japan with the U.S. Air Force and attained the rank of shihan (master instructor) in hakkoryu jujutsu in 1963. Professor Palumbo has also studied several styles of karate, earning a third degree black belt in the shotokan style. He started the Hakkoryu Martial Arts Federation in 1974 to promote the arts of both ju-jutsu and karate.

According to Palumbo, the philosophy of hakkoryu is one of humane control of attackers by the utilization of the pain inflicted through the use of pressure point strikes and holds. The pain is intense but only momentary in order to allow the practitioner to subdue an attacker. Hakkoryu, like many other Japanese martial arts, also makes use of *shiatsu,* a form of finger pressure massage, for the treatment of injuries and for overall physical well-being.

I personally like ju-jutsu though," he adds, "because it's (strictly) a self-defense.

"I've found that for the amount of time that people put into the martial arts they can get more out of ju-jutsu than they can out of karate. After six months' time in karate, at least in the traditional kind of karate that I do, you will still be punching and kicking, doing the basics. In fact, you'll still be doing that at a year. In ju-jutsu, however, you will be learning how to twist the wrist, how to escape. In ju-jutsu in six months, which is about the average span of time that most people get involved in the martial arts, they have gotten their money's worth."

Craig is quick to point out, however, that no one can expect to be a self-defense expert in only six months.

"In that amount of time all I can hope to teach them is a trick or two. It's a fact of life that the longer you stay the better you become. Some instructors breed what I call false courage into their students. You know, 'If you do this and that then you will be able to go out into the street and whip any person.' They go out into the street and try it and get wiped out. I feel sorry for them. I don't lie to my students."

Barry Gimbellot is also an experienced instructor, with black belts in ju-jutsu and in tae kwon-do. He disagrees with Craig that you are stuck with learning the basics in karate for the first year and never get to the more practical self-defense techniques.

"That may be the way they teach in Japan, but not in American karate or tae kwon-do schools. I teach even beginning students a bit of both karate and ju-jutsu techniques."

It is Gimbellot's opinion that ju-jutsu is harder to learn, at least initially, than karate or tae kwon-do.

"For regular self-defense," he says, "I prefer the so-called escape and destroy techniques of tae kwon-do. I think they are more applicable to most situations. I'd rather give the guy a good strong side kick than try to do a wrist-lock on him. However, I think that the *controls* of ju-jutsu are much better [than karate], but they take five times the amount of training [to do properly] than escape and destroy does. You mess up on a control any little bit and the person gets away from you and you have a potentially dangerous situation on your hands. Wrist-locks and throws are, for the most part, harder to perform and so they take longer to learn. The more complicated something is, the more of a chance for messing up. It's a lot easier to just punch or kick somebody."

Dennis Palumbo is one of the few Americans to attain the official title of *shihan* (master instructor) in *hakkoryu* ju-jutsu. He also has earned his black belt in three different styles of karate. He believes that the more varied responses of ju-jutsu make it more practical than karate.

"Our theory of self-defense [in hakkoryu] is to inflict a minimum amount of pain or physical damage to an attacker. The whole idea is to relax and not use strength, as in karate.

Fig. 24 Jukoryu ju-jutsu expert, Dr. Ted Gambordella, shows his *ki* force by bending two sharp knives against his neck. Developed by breathing exercises and concentration drills, ki is used by some ju-jutsu stylists to allow them to receive blows in the stomach, ribs, neck, and even groin without injury.

Therefore I won't let my students take both karate and ju-jutsu because it would be too confusing," says Palumbo.

Steve Weiss is of the same opinion, saying, "In karate it's basically punch-kick-block-strike and you practice so much at it that you get so good nothing else is necessary, and that is the essence of karate. In ju-jutsu you are more flexible with your mind and with your body so that you can adapt to any situation, whether you're on the ground grappling, where a joint-lock or strangle might be necessary, or in a standing situation where you could do a body throw or strike."

Wally Jay is a well-known ju-jutsu master from Alameda, California, who has come up with what he calls his "small circle theory." He says that by reducing the circular motion in certain wrist and arm locks the techniques can be executed faster and more effectively. He says the idea of ju-jutsu controls is to administer the proper amount of pain. Too much pain and the attacker is likely to be injured, but too little gives him the opportunity to punch or kick his way out of the hold.

If an attacker does manage to slip out of the hold, Jay says that there are plenty of other holds he can easily shift into.

"We don't punch or kick too much," he admits. "In tang soo do or karate, once a practitioner gets in close, he doesn't know what to do. That's where my type of techniques come in."

Like Darryl Craig, Dennis Palumbo says that he talks to his prospective students about both karate and ju-jutsu, although his own personal favorite is ju-jutsu. Hakkoryu style was founded in 1941 by Okuyama Yoshiharu and has been described as a soft style that stresses relaxed and varied techniques rather than rigid preset responses. The students first learn the techniques from a sitting position *(seiza waza)* before they learn the subtle footwork encountered in standing self-defense techniques *(tachi waza)*.

I asked Palumbo if he had encountered any hard styles of ju-jutsu.

"Sure, one of the best examples is *jukoryu.* They are a hard style that uses what they call 'high-level ki' where they can take blows to the body and even the throat. We don't do things like that at all. I believe that if it takes a person fifteen or twenty seconds to prepare for a blow to the throat, then it's more a demonstration than a self-defense. I believe in a more immediate type of technique."

But Ted Gambordella, a jukoryu stylist, says, "I don't need any preparation to do my hard ki. Sacharnoski didn't need any preparation either." (Rod Sacharnoski was the founder of this hard style which places emphasis on ki as a means to withstand full power blows to the unprotected body.) "Now when he was doing dangerous hard ki, he did prepare. Everyone wanted to see how far you could stretch it. We started out getting hit in the ribs, the stomach, or the throat and no one else could do that. Then someone would say, 'How about the back of the neck? How about the eye? How about the groin?' Then they started hitting him with baseball bats. Now, that's just showmanship, and that's not necessary or very practical, I will admit. [Fred] Defelice [another jukoryu master] had to prepare himself when he would hold both arms out and have two people side kick him at one time. He would let people poke him in the eyes. He told me himself that at the time he didn't know if it would work and just how far he could actually go. I've seen him get hit in the neck by four guys all over 200 pounds from all sides at the same time. I've seen Sacharnoski get kicked so hard in the groin that it would lift him into the air. I've seen them break a baseball bat on his ribs; in fact, I've even done that," says Gambordella.

"When I first got into ju-jutsu, that's what I was in it for, the ki. But now the ki means nothing to me. It just keeps my body strong. That's not the art, it's just showmanship. It's like brick-breaking in karate. It's fun, and people like to see it, but it doesn't mean a thing really. It's just something you do in a demonstration to get people's attention so they will want to take up the art.

"Ju-jutsu is a way of life, a philosophy," continues Gambordella. "It's a method for me to teach others something that will make them better people, physically, mentally, and spiritually. The direct influence you have on someone to make them achieve the potential they have is what makes you a master. It's not how many boards you can break or how many tournaments you've won. A master has the ability to change the lives of his students. If I can do hard ki but I can't teach anyone else to do it, then it's no good."

George Kirby also believes in the philosophy of ju-jutsu. He believes that the destructive potential of the art requires a strong emphasis on the concept of nonviolence.

"Our style is called *budoshin*," Kirby told me, "and we teach honor and respect." He says that it is humanly degrading to become involved in an actual physical confrontation because it indicates that reason and intelligence have failed.

Kirby says that mental calmness and alertness will not only enable you to talk your way out of a dangerous situation, but it can help you fight your way out of it if all else has failed.

"When you are calm and in control of your mind and body," he says, "your techniques will be smoother and you can perform almost effortlessly."

The smoothness of a student's performance is one thing instructors look for in advancing a person in ju-jutsu. There is kata in ju-jutsu, but it is unlike that found in karate.

"A kata is sometimes only a simple takedown," says Kirby. "Waza is a whole series of kata together, perhaps locking techniques or holds or striking techniques. You are generally expected to know certain kata for advancement, but you also have to know how to defend against certain attacks. It is up to the individual as to which kata or technique to use.

"Some styles have tournaments," says Kirby, "where the students can do what they call free-style kata where there is an attacker and a defender. The attacker can do any technique he wishes to do and we see how well the defender responds to the attack with his ju-jutsu techniques. The attacker cannot resist any technique the person throws and must go with any defensive move, so there are certain safeguards built in, much as in karate competition. You have to have rules to keep people from getting hurt," Kirby points out.

Aiki-jutsu, one of the old ju-jutsu styles, holds an annual world championship in Tokyo, Japan. Both in 1981 and 1982 an American won the championship, an almost unheard of feat, especially for an American. He won the free-style competition, the open forms competition, the weapons competition, and placed second in the six man self-defense competition. His name is Bill Hancock, and he told me that the aiki-jutsu tournaments are knock-down drag-out affairs.

"Normally you cannot compete in advanced hard randori [fighting] until you are a black belt because you have to know what you are doing. If you feel someone putting pressure on a joint and you resist and don't go with it, you could end up with your hand hanging on a thread!"

Hancock is a bear of a man who holds a black belt in aikido in addition to aiki-jutsu, and he is presently working on his black belt in tae kwon-do as well.

"In karate (tae kwon-do) I find everybody wants to kill and maim. I used to be that way myself, but my aiki-jutsu teacher, Mr. Yamashita, showed me that nonaggression is a better way. In this art the more aggressive you are, the more you're going to catch it."

But Hancock admits that sometimes you might need *both* the soft and yielding approach of ju-jutsu or aikido and the bone crunching power of karate.

"I was working in downtown Dallas at the newspaper late one night, and as I was walking to my car three men tried to relieve me of my wallet," he told me. "I used a combination of aiki-jutsu and karate and put them all in the hospital. The first guy came at me with a knife and, rather than trying a hard block which I'm sure would have cut my arm, I went with it and then brought it back and snapped his wrist, a very basic move. Then I kicked the next guy with a karate kick. Some people will tell you that *their* art is all you need to know, but I've found a combination of arts really works well."

Ju-jutsu is by no means the perfect art, but it does have some of the best parts of several arts combined in a single system. I have found it to be an enjoyable addition to my tae kwon-do training. As with any martial art, however, you'll need to be ready to devote a lot of time and effort to mastering its varied and sophisticated techniques.

Judo

Jigoro Kano grew up in the latter half of the nineteenth century in Japan. He had been a sickly child and had taken up ju-jutsu mainly for its physical benefits. Kano was an astute observer of both the martial and cultural scenes in Japan. He valued the physical and mental discipline that ju-jutsu embodied, but he knew that in order to popularize it he would need to eliminate some of the more lethal aspects and concentrate on a more scientific approach to teaching principles of leverage and balance. By 1882 he had developed a new discipline which he called judo ("the gentle way" or "the flexible way").

Kano's first school was called the Kodokan, but still was considered another style of ju-jutsu until 1886 when the Tokyo Metropolitan Police Board staged a tournament between the Kodokan and the Totsuka, the largest of the ju-jutsu schools. The Kodokan stylists won thirteen and tied two of the fifteen matches, and from that time on Kodokan judo became known as a separate art.

Kano himself stressed that his art was different saying,

"Many ju-jutsu schools indulged in dangerous practices such as throwing by rather unfair means or by wrenching limbs. Add to this that there were several ill-disciplined ju-jutsu schools where the pupils themselves were obnoxious to the public by willingly throwing down innocent people or seeking quarrels. Some gave exhibitions of their art by making their disciples battle wrestlers, charging a fee for admission. These amateur showmen became the object of amusement and quite naturally earned public scorn and disgrace. The situation, then, was really such that I was led to think that my own system, if taught under the name ju-jutsu, might prove unacceptable to persons of the higher classes. Hence the adoption of the word *judo*."

Although it contains many of the throwing, choking, and joint-locking techniques of ju-jutsu, its strict set of rules and guiding principles makes it primarily a sport rather than a combat art. Judo was recognized as an Olympic sport in 1964, and achieved status as a popular international activity.

Vince Tamura is a seventh dan in judo. He is a former world class competitor and was chosen as one of the first olympic officials for the 1964 Tokyo Olympic Games.

"Like ju-jutsu, judo is based on a circle. In judo you use your opponent's strength to your advantage. A lot of that comes by giving way or yielding. Also someone may get themselves out of position or off-balance and then you can apply your techniques.

"In judo you have eight directions in which you can make your attack," Tamura told me. "You have front and rear and side to side and also the corners. All your throws come from one of these directions, whether it be foot throws, hip throws, or sacrifice throws, which is where you drop to your back or side to gain an advantage over your opponent."

One of the first things you do in judo class is work on your falling techniques or *ukemi*.

"In the very first lesson we teach the falls, and a lot of

people pick it up very fast," Tamura points out. "We don't rush into actually throwing too soon. They do a lot of falls by themselves first, roll-outs, backwards falls, side falls, and so on. Once they have that and we know their balance is good we go ahead and let them throw."

Because of the emphasis on throwing, judo dojos all have mats. Judo practitioners must all wear the judogi, which is made of a much heavier material than karate uniforms to stand up to the pulling and tugging of competition.

Anson Shupe is a sociology professor at the University of Texas at Arlington. He has earned his black belt in both judo and karate.

"Judo is to wrestling as karate is to boxing," he claims. "One is more concerned with grappling control, using limbs in a grabbing manner, and the other is more concerned with striking and blocking.

"When I started karate," says Dr. Shupe, "I had fantasies that I would be able to integrate a lot of my judo, but the only judo I really was able to integrate was foot sweeps, where you sweep a forward foot if the weight is committed, like in a straddle stance. But against an upper belt that even isn't so good, because once they know you're going to sweep their foot, they will go with it and bring the foot around and hit you with a heel kick. So that only works on a black belt once or twice and then he sees that's your technique and you're going to get a foot in your ribs. Of course, on a blue belt or brown belt you could do it all night.

"The reason it doesn't work—the reason judo is not easily assimilated into sparring—and we are talking about sparring here because I believe the two can be worked out in self-defense very easily—is that the karate person is trained to strike in the most efficient way, basically a straight line with no wild roundhouse-type punches. Judo depends on a person coming at you with either outstretched arms or with a wild swing. Someone who knows how to punch in a very tight straight line is never going to make the kinds of moves that are easy to seize. Unless the person hangs a punch or kick-out, which a karate person isn't supposed to do," says Shupe, "a judo person won't have enough time to grab it. In a sparring situation karate is just too fast.

"The classic question, of course, is in a fight between judo and karate, who is going to win. I think the judo guy will have to absorb a kick or punch—that is, stop it—long enough to grab it. Then he could do something.

"Now, I think judo has some superior moves that karate people don't seem to learn, like how to fight on your back," says Shupe. "Karate people really aren't that good on the ground. Judo does have atemi waza, or striking techniques, which are only taught to brown belts and above, and it's really just simplistic karate. But judo guys usually don't work on it. I think that more judo people pick up on karate techniques than karate people pick up on judo techniques, though."

Even though strikes are not allowed in judo competition, you can get hit, Shupe warns. He reaches out to hold my lapel to demonstrate.

"In international rules, if I am holding onto your gi and hit you, like this," and he jams his fist into my chest, "then that's legal because it's part of the throw.

"For instance, in a tournament I used to grab my opponent's gi at the back of his neck and give him a jerk to hit the base of his skull and give him a little whiplash to get his mind off the hip throw. A number of throws depend on pushing, and it's inevitable that you're going to hit them, but if you're holding onto the gi that makes it a legal part of the throw."

I asked Dr. Shupe if he thought judo was taught more as a sport than a self-defense art.

"Well, after the Americans got hold of it, yeah. We've made it into a big tournament thing. It was originally meant to be more philosophical, to be more of a self-improvement, stressing mastery of your body, physical and mental development and so forth, which of course any good martial art should do.

"Kano had two principles," Dr. Shupe continues. "One was a maximum efficiency with a minimum of effort (known as *seiryoku zenyo*) and the other was mutual improvement of yourself and the people you work out with *(juta kyoei)*. It was meant to be friendlier than the karate classes I see where people argue about who got who. In judo there's not much question anyway, because either you got the throw or you didn't.

"I think I could defend the assertion that it is more of a sport," says Shupe. "I was the vice president of the Midwest Judo Association and both a coach and a competitor. That was before the NCAA took over. Once they did and set up strict AAU rules, I could never accept a dime for teaching because once I did I couldn't participate in any AAU matches, which meant I could never get promoted."

One of the requirements for higher ranks is knowing how to resuscitate someone in case of unconsciousness. Judo chokes are very effective and could be dangerous. Even though you are supposed to tap the mat to indicate that you are close to blacking out, some people don't do it in time, preferring to try and struggle a bit longer.

"You can knock someone out in a matter of seconds and then of course kill them, but the chokes are designed not to break the neck, but to render someone unconscious," says Shupe.

"You're allowed to tap with your feet if you have to, but sometimes it happens so fast, and the guy doesn't react and tap, and he could be out for quite a while. Most of the time just moving their head around gets them out of it, but sometimes you have to slap them in the face. I saw one tournament where a guy went out and everybody was just standing around and didn't know what to do, and this Korean came in and *bam*, hit him. Sometimes you sit him up. It all depends on how long he's been out."

Speaking of training injuries, Shupe says "I consider judo more dangerous than karate, because karate people are more aware of their lethal potential. They know that if you hit someone in the throat it's all over, and so they take more pains controlling themselves. In a judo tournament people don't want to take a safe fall because it makes a big thud and you are more likely to lose a full point (ippon) and lose the match. If you take a poor fall, the other guy may only get a half-point and the match is still on. Also, in America you follow them down and fall on top of them knocking their wind out so they won't want to fight anymore. I had to unlearn that when I trained in Japan because they consider that poor sportsmanship and you won't get the point. In America they say, 'Hey, great hard throw.' In Japan they say, 'That's a terrible throw, you lost your balance and fell on him.'"

To the question of how long it takes to learn how to defend yourself using judo techniques, Shupe answers, "I'm tempted to say half a year but I've known guys who have had just a month of judo and they've gone to a bar where somebody has pushed them or something and they threw him over their hip and really looked like a bad dude. I'd have to say that if you only had four weeks to train, you could learn a whole lot more karate than judo but, on the other hand, you could never get the flexibility that it takes to do a lot of the karate moves well in just four weeks either.

"In all, judo has forty-eight basic throws, each of which has several variations, it's got several dozen chokes, at least a dozen arm locks, well over a dozen different combinations of mat holds. Karate is more like kendo, you learn the basics fairly fast. In judo you may get to be a brown belt and there are still half the techniques that you haven't learned. That's what strikes me as a real difference between judo and karate.

In karate there are relatively few basic techniques and everything else is combinations. In judo an awfully lot of the
throws don't resemble anything else, there's no carry-over.

"You can teach the person a lot of moves in judo if they
didn't have to take the falls," continues Shupe. "In other
words, if you didn't have to be the dummy you could learn a
lot. What takes such a long time in judo is that everybody
takes turns being the *tori,* the thrower, and the *uke,* the
follower. If you never had to worry about learning how to
fall you could learn a lot faster."

Vince Tamura points out that there are rigid formal
methods by which you must work on your falling and throwing techniques. These are the judo *kata.*

"It is all prearranged with your partner. The tori per-
forms the throws and the uke takes the falls," says Tamura.
"Nage-no-kata takes in prearranged throwing techniques.
The grappling kata is *katame-no-kata.* There are other katas
for black belt as well."

Rank is based on both knowledge of the art and proficiency in tournaments. The founder of judo, professor Kano,
devised the *kyu-dan* ranking system, which is today used in
most other martial arts. The kyu grades start with white belt
and go through yellow, orange, green, blue, and brown belts.
Dan ranks go from first degree, black belt, the lowest, to
tenth degree, the highest. Sixth through eighth dan wear red
and white belts, ninth and tenth wear red belts. The twelfth
dan, which only Kano held, was signified by a white belt,
showing he had transcended the ranking system which he
created.

Despite its colorful history and its success as an international sport, judo seems to be on the decline in the United
States. Says Anson Shupe, "I started in 1964, and back then
karate seemed to be looked at as kind of lower class and
seedy. Judo, on the other hand, got into the YMCA quickly.
There were several judo dojos in the city of Pittsburgh back

then but only one karate school that I know of. Judo resembled wrestling so much and there was so much etiquette and rigid rules that it seemed to reassure the powers that be that, although there was a possibility of injury, it looked a lot more under control than karate."

Nowadays that situation seems to have reversed itself. Look in the Yellow Pages of most cities and you will see several karate, tae kwon-do, and even kung fu schools listed, but only one or two judo dojos—if you are lucky.

"I think from the standpoint of physical fitness, karate is superior," says Shupe. "If you want to work out by yourself in judo you do shadow *ikami,* kind of a shadow wrestling [which is] very unsatisfying and very unrealistic, and so most guys don't even bother to do it. But in karate you can do the majority of all your techniques from stretching to combinations alone. I found I got tired of needing a mat and a body or partner. I don't know if that's the major reason, but judo is definitely on the decline in popularity.

"One of the things that's so discouraging for women is they think they'll learn some self-defense and so they get into judo and then realize it's going to be a long time before they can do anything to anybody, much less a bigger man. Put a woman in a karate class, though, and she can learn how to kick a guy in the groin fairly quickly. She can see the utility.

"Judo is kind of messy," Shupe continues. "It's not that glamorous. It's like wrestling. Karate is more spectacular, more Hollywood. It's not that there isn't sweat in both arts, but in judo you've got your head between somebody's legs."

Bob Woerner is a black belt in Korean tae kwon-do who decided several years ago to broaden his training by taking up judo. I asked him about the difference between the two arts in a self-defense situation.

"First off let me say that judo is an extremely valid self-defense. It is as rough as it can be. All you really need is to get ahold of someone and do one simple throw and he is

O-U-T. I mean you are dropping him three, four, five feet and with his whole weight, plus the inertia that you put into it, it can be just devastating. To be dropped on the street when you didn't expect it would wipe anybody out.

"Here's the bad thing though," Woerner continues. "At a distance judo is worthless. You have to really be involved in the fracas. In judo it's a situation where you might have to take some licks up front. You will have a guy swing on you and have gotten into some kind of entanglement before your judo comes into play. In karate you can stop it at a distance. In judo you have to know a lot of different things that you don't have to learn in karate. You don't have to have flexibility but you do need upper body strength. You have to be able to move your feet very quickly too," Woerner observes. "Judo, with its chokes and all, is kind of like a boa constrictor approach, whereas karate is like a cobra strike. They'll both get you but in a different way."

Aikido

In 1917, Morihei Ueshiba earned his teaching license in the *daito ryu* style of *aiki-jutsu* (one of the first ju-jutsu styles). Daito ryu was known for its emphasis on the use of circular motions in self-defense (much like some of the softer Chinese systems). As judo's founder, Jigoro Kano, had concluded only a few years earlier, Ueshiba saw that propagating a combat-oriented art in modern Japanese society would be increasingly difficult. O-sensei, as Ueshiba is called, was an extremely religious individual and valued highly the ethical and spiritual principles that were to be found in *budo* (the martial ways of Japan).

So, during the 1920s, Ueshiba formulated his sophisticated art of evasion and nonviolent self-defense, which he called aikido (way of divine harmony). Aikido is the most internal of the Japanese arts, with a strong emphasis on the concept of *ki*, or universal energy. Special breathing exercises and meditation techniques taken from Zen Buddhism are integral parts of aikido's ki training.

Ueshiba designed aikido as a purely defensive art and therefore discouraged the notion of free-form sparring or competition. He emphasized throwing and joint techniques instead of striking and kicking. Aikido's primary aim is a healthy mind and body controlled by a calm and righteous spirit.

Unlike judo, which has retained the regimentation of its founder, aikido has splintered into several substyles. Most of the difference lies in the philosophical approach rather than with the actual techniques themselves.

It was during the late 1940s and 1950s that several of Ueshiba's students ventured out to develop their own systems. Kenji Tomiki had studied judo for many years before his introduction to aikido. He decided to introduce a sporting or competitive element while still retaining the basic prin-

Fig. 25 Properly executed aikido throws (done here by Bill Sosa) look almost fake because of the ease with which the master can send his opponents through the air. Aikido stylists wear a hakama, a dresslike lower garment, over their gi-pants.

ciples. *Tomiki aikido* is very popular in modern Japan.

Yoshin aikido was founded by Gozo Shioda, who had spent many years acting as Ueshiba's *uke* (the recipient of the technique). Perhaps because of that Shioda's style is sometimes referred to as the "hard style" of aikido, coming closer to the old ju-jutsu style of aiki-jutsu in its approach to execution of technique, even including some atemi (striking) techniques. Although yoshin aikido places much less emphasis on ki than does Ueshiba style, it retains the spiritual purposes, in order to teach harmony of mind and body. It also stresses that aikido is a way of life rather than just a physical art form.

Keijutsukai aikido was founded in 1979 by (Hawaiian) Thomas Makiyama in Tokyo, Japan. Makiyama is an eighth degree black belt and officially certified *shihan* (master instructor) of aikido. He became frustrated with what he calls "unrealistic" training in the softer approaches, citing theoretical rather than practical attack and defense patterns.

Speaking about the Ueshiba style in his book, he states, "The school is also a proponent of the so-called ki principle, where concentration is allegedly centered at a point just below the navel, resulting in a spiritual source of undefined strength necessary in the execution of aikido movements and techniques . . . students are erroneously led to believe that a mystical source of spiritual power lies at the root of aikido, and that this particular concept must be mastered through a prescribed form of concentration which borders on Zen Buddhism." Makiyama maintains that aikido is based on principles of elementary physics.

There are several other sects of aikido, but, since you are very unlikely to run across them, we will move on to the basic principles of aikido movement.

In aikido, body movement is coordinated in such a way that the power of the defender is harmonized with (or joined with) the incoming power of the attacker. The force is thus directed harmlessly past the intended victim and is turned back on the unsuspecting attacker. The basic principle is circular movement. Since most attacks come in a straight line, it is as if the attacker is drawn into a centrifuge and then thrown off.

"In a way it is similar to the sticky hands kung fu movements," says Bill Hancock, a black belt in aikido as well as aiki-jutsu. "It's similar in that the idea is to be able to control the flow of your opponent. An *irimi* is an entering movement where you let the person go by you by continuing the flow. *Tenkan* is a kind of a reverse motion movement where you enter and I reverse the motion on you to take you down. I'm still working in a circular fashion, but by reversing the motion I'm introducing a violent change. When using tenkan movements you need to be very careful or you'll hurt someone pretty bad."

"In aikido we train a lot on timing," says Bill Sosa, a high ranking sensei from Dallas. "You must move at the proper time. It's kind of like pulling a chair out from under someone just as he starts to sit down. His commitment has been made, he is already moving, and all you have to do is pull the chair away. You *blend* with his movement.

"We do have mostly circular movements," Sosa continues, "but we have straight-line moves too. You can't always move in a circle. Let's say you are in a telephone booth and there's only one way to get out and that's in a straight line. If you are doing *randori,* which is our free-style, against multiple attacks and you just move in a circle, you will have to move into one of your attackers and that wouldn't make sense."

Over the years aikido has gotten the reputation of being more of an art form or sport than a practical self-defense.

"Aikido and judo were designed as sports," says ju-jutsu master Dennis Palumbo. "I have several aikido people as students, one almost ready for black belt (in aikido), and he said to me, 'You know, I still haven't learned much self-defense.' That's just not what it is designed for."

While it is true that Ueshiba's aikido emphasized mind/body unification and ethical principles to a greater degree than do most other martial arts, aikido masters naturally don't agree that it is an ineffective self-defense.

"That kind of statement indicates a lack of knowledge about aikido," counters Bill Sosa. "Maybe they have seen a class or two where we are training people the basics of how to move, blending, how to take someone down gently. Let me tell you a true story to illustrate.

"My son, Ric, teaches aikido in Mexico," says Sosa. "There was a guy there who was watching Ric teach for several nights in a row. He had been teaching just the basics like how to blend, how to harmonize, balance, gentle takedowns, things like that. Apparently the guy finally decided to challenge Ric. He had just finished teaching a class—talking about the nonviolent aspect of aikido and so forth—when this guy tells him he's going to kick his butt. Of course Ric tried to dissuade the guy but he wouldn't listen. So after he takes off his coat and shoes he rushes my son with a punch. Ric sweeps him and on the way down he hits him with a punch and knocks most of his teeth out. The guy is out cold and Ric takes him by the hair and throws him out into the street. When the guy finally comes to he was asking everybody why Ric hit him. 'He teaches aikido—they aren't supposed to hit!' he kept saying."

"I'm telling you this," says Sosa, "so you will realize that aikido is as effective as you want to make it, as destructive as you want to make it. We just don't go overboard like some [arts] who advocate smashing the guy's head in while he's down. That's what most people want to do anyway, they want to fight. We teach proper awareness, balance, energy flow, not just fighting.

PROFILE

Fig. 26 Morris K. Sasaki is the head instructor for *keijutsukai aikido* in the United States. He has been involved in the martial arts for eighteen years and has taught self-defense classes for women, for the elderly, and for the Lennox, California, Sheriff's department. Sasaki Sensei is a registered physical therapist and currently instructs a self-protection program for persons with disABILITIES. "I started this class in response to the increased crime against this somewhat vulnerable population,' he says. "All class members must have a medical clearance, including an M.D.'s approval and a physical therapy screening evaluation. We take into account the specific medical diagnoses of each individual and try to maximize each person's ABILITIES."

Fig. 26-B Sasaki Sensei is flipped after applying a choke hold on a paraplegic friend at the Daniel Freeman Memorial Hospital in Inglewood, California.

Fig. 27 Makiyama Shihan, the founder of keijutsukai aikido, effortlessly tosses two opponents to the ground.

"If I take you down and hold you," continues Sosa, "you will not get up. I can punch you, gouge out your eyes, anything I want. But people don't see that, they just say 'they go soft in practice.'

"Most people don't believe it anyway. They say, 'Aw, he's throwing himself.' I was one of those. I didn't believe in aikido when I first saw a demonstration in Chicago years ago," admits Sosa, who was already a black belt in karate at the time. "This fellow was leading his opponents and taking them down and the first thing that came to my mind was 'that's not going to work in a street situation.' And, you know, it won't work that way, but if you try to grab my wrist and I know how to punch or execute a *hard* throw, then it will work. If I just try to lead you around and around, of course you aren't going to hang onto my wrist that long. Who's going to stick out his arm and let himself be led and then be gently thrown away? We just train that way in order to understand the basics."

"The Tokyo police require some martial arts training," says Morris Sasaki, from the Torrance, California, headquarters of the keijutsukai style in America. "They can train in kendo, judo, or aikido. Aikido is included because its techniques are effective even though they are not offensive. Other martial arts are quite offensive, but you do not attack with aikido. We use just control techniques. But if the *arm* is under control, the whole body is under control," Sasaki points out. "That's what makes aikido different from other martial arts. It is control and countermovements, no attacks."

If there is a weakness in using aikido for self-defense, it would have to be that rigidly defined and purely defensive way of practicing. Bryan Robbins was a third degree black belt in tae kwon-do when he started his aikido training several years ago. He evaluated the two arts for me.

"If a person's training was only in aikido, then they

would not be used to seeing a variety of strikes like backfists, front kicks, round kicks, stuff like that. I think they would also be susceptible to fakes because much of their defenses are based on avoiding just a single attack. So as far as real self-defense on the street, where you can't talk your way out of the situation, a person who is trained in karate would do a better job (than an aikido stylist). When you concentrate on defense exclusively you think defensively. In karate you think offensively, like how to hurt someone."

Robbins was quick to add a counterbalance to that, however.

"I think a person who has studied aikido, though, is less apt to get into a fight than a person who has studied karate because of its noncompetitive nature. That in itself is reason enough to train in aikido."

Robbins was an Olympic level competitive diver and then a coach for the United States Olympic Team. He presently is a professor of physical education for Southern Methodist University.

"I've been competitive all my life, all the way to the Olympics, which is as competitive as you can get. I got to the point where I was tired of constantly trying to prove myself. That gets to be a drag after a while. I like doing aikido just for the physical enjoyment of it. It's a different mindset [from karate]. That's not to say there aren't any people in karate like that, but there are more in aikido."

"Aikido doesn't have that competitive spirit," agrees Sasaki. "The American way is competition, and you succeed by winning. Aikido does not have that. You compete only with yourself, and that is sometimes difficult for people to understand." Mr. Sasaki believes that is one reason aikido is not as popular as karate in this country.

"Karate techniques are easier to learn," reflects Sosa. "With a front snap kick or roundhouse kick, you can see what you are doing even if there is no one else there. In aikido you need a partner. Also there's so many angles that it just takes longer [to learn]. I would have to say that you could be effective in karate in a shorter period of time."

Bill Hancock believes that karate people would do well to learn some aikido techniques, however. Specifically he cites the falling and rolling techniques.

"I know karate guys who never think about it. In the karate school where I work out, for example, no one likes to fall, so when we do demonstrations, guess who gets to be the dummy? I'm the only one who knows how to fall properly. Knowing that can save your life in the street. Let's just say you happen to slip and fall, which is very possible, really. If you don't know how to protect yourself you could really get hurt. That is part of the basic training of aikido and judo and some of those arts. Karate doesn't teach that," says Hancock.

"Imagine a karate guy throwing a side kick on the street. He slips and falls and he'll probably hurt something because he doesn't know how to fall properly. He'll tense up, freeze, go *boom* on the pavement, and while he lies there, out of commission, his opponent is going to stomp him."

Aikido does indeed have a lot to offer the martial arts student, like how to fall and how to tumble when you find yourself off balance. The balance awareness and mental concentration can also be quite helpful. I know I have enjoyed the limited amount of aikido training I have had. However, because of its sophistication, both mental and physical, and because of its purely defensive approach to self-defense, I would say it might be more suited as a secondary art for the average person just wishing to learn how to defend himself in the shortest period of time. But if you want to get involved in an activity that develops your mind/body coordination, your overall awareness, and a spirit of nonviolence, and you are willing to devote some time to it, then aikido could be the art for you.

Ju-jutsu against a choke

Ju-jutsu expert Ted Gambordella is grabbed in a front choke.

He reaches across with his right hand. Note his left hand grabbing the attacker's elbow.

This closeup reveals how Gambordella has lifted up the little finger.

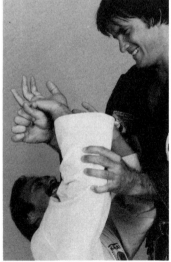

Now he bends the finger back, driving the opponent to his knees.

Ju-jutsu against a punch

Gambordella blocks an incoming punch to begin a typical ju-jutsu defense.

He immediately does an open-handed throat strike/grab.

Gambordella has reached around his opponent's waist and stepped in . . .

to execute a hip throw.

He can now drop his right knee into his opponent's chest, do a punch, or a stomp, or whatever he desires.

Ju-jutsu against a punch

Sidestepping this punching attack, Gambordella blocks with an open hand and grabs his opponent's hand.

A front kick to the groin is executed while still holding onto the attacker's hand.

Now using both hands . . .

he drops his attacker with a wrist throw.

A stomp to the face finishes up the defense.

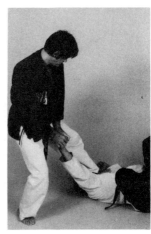

Judo against a punch

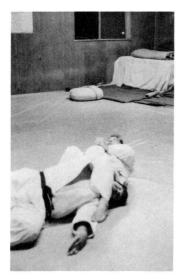

Tamura here blocks an incoming punch . . .

and shifts his body around.

Bending his knees for leverage . . .

he executes a shoulder throw.

Now, as the attacker is on the ground . . .

he steps over his head . . .

and drops into a typical judo pin.

Judo against a choke

Judo master Vince Tamura is grabbed in
a front choke.

He reaches up and over with his left arm
while holding the opponent's hand
tightly with his right.

Tamura pivots around, pulling the
attacker off balance.

He now applies a judo arm lock.

Close-up.

Judo against a choke

Tamura is choked again.

He grasps his opponent's jacket and leans back.

With his foot in the attacker's stomach, he falls to the ground . . .

and flips him up and over.

Aikido against a choke

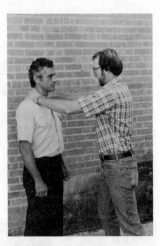

Aikido sensei Bill Sosa is grabbed from
the front by Bryan Robbins.

A close-up reveals how Sosa reaches up
to grasp his opponent's thumb.

Now, using the other hand, he twists
his attacker's hand.

Putting pressure on the wrist . . .

he forces his opponent to the ground.

Aikido against a punch

Sosa stands calmly as his attacker
threatens.

He steps in swiftly as the opponent starts
his own move.

Placing one hand under the chin and the
other on his attacker's shoulder . . .

he steps through and forces the
opponent to the ground.

Because aikido is purely defensive, a
follow-up punch or kick is usually
not advocated.

CHAPTER SEVEN

Training Secrets

The Scientific Approach

This chapter is not for the person only interested in *reading* about the warrior arts. It is for the actual practitioner of one of the various systems we have discussed so far. It is said that there are two things that make a champion—ability and knowledge. I believe that you can't really improve your physical abilities by reading a book (although hopefully you have been inspired by reading this one to go out and seek to improve yours), but you can certainly increase your knowledge by researching various sources.

I've done that for you here by talking with experts in the areas of nutrition, sports psychology, physiology, and weight training. These are the areas that American martial artists have increasingly turned to to improve their competitive edge. As a result, the Americans are recognized as world leaders in the new, scientific aspects of the age-old warrior arts.

Muscles and Stretching

Being primarily a Korean stylist, I was trained in the high and powerful kicks characteristic of that style. Chuck Norris credits his early tournament success to his ability to score on his Japanese schooled opponents with his Korean-style spinning kicks, something he still likes to do in his films. As American karate has progressed, everybody has seen the importance of kicking ability. Witness the fact that Bill Wallace, who started out in the low-kicking Okinawan school, became known as "Superfoot" due to his incredibly high and fast left-footed kicks. In the kata divisions, world-recognized champions like George Chung are the ones who can kick higher and harder than anyone else. Wallace, Chung, and other kicking champions stress the importance of regular stretching exercises.

It isn't just karate people that need to stretch. When I started my aikido classes, I expected the circular motion drills and the falling and rolling exercises, but I was mildly

154

surprised by the stretching routines that the sensei had us do. I guess I shouldn't have been, really, because flexibility is a very important factor, not only for the proper execution of any physical technique. It has also been proven to be an important factor in the prevention of athletic injuries.

"Flexibility is specific to each joint," says Bryan Robbins, a physical education professor, former Olympic coach and third degree black belt in tae kwon-do. "For instance you can be flexible in your shoulders and inflexible in your hamstrings, or vice versa. In some of the studies they've done, they've discovered if you do the same action over and over again without stopping, like running, then those muscles will tend to shorten. So martial artists who do a lot of running to get their cardiovascular endurance would be well advised to stretch a lot."

Before we discuss actual stretching exercises and precautions to take, it might be helpful to examine the makeup of the muscles themselves. The word *muscle* comes from the Latin word for mouse, because, like a mouse, a muscle has a body with a tail, the tendon that attaches it to a bone.

Skeletal muscles, which are the ones that do the work when you move your body, are made up of two different kinds of muscle fibers called by scientists *slow-twitch* and *fast-twitch*. Slow-twitch fibers are used for prolonged or aerobic work; fast-twitch fibers are used in strength and power activities. Studies indicate that long distance runners, for example, have a high number of slow-twitch muscle fibers, while sprinters have a high number of fast-twitch fibers.

"Everybody is born with a certain combination of fast-twitch and slow-twitch muscle fibers," says Robbins. "You can never change it, it's kind of like fingerprints. People with fast-twitch fibers tend to gravitate towards fast-type activities that require explosive motions, and those with slow-twitch are probably better in sports that contain longer periods of activity.

"There is a vertical jump test for determining the kind of muscle fibers you have," says Robbins. "Stand next to a wall and see how high you can jump. Try not to bend your knees too much or use your arms. Some marathoners can only jump twelve inches or so, but some sprinters can jump thirty inches."

"I wouldn't be too concerned with what kind of muscle fibers you have, though," says Paul Hinkley, another physical education instructor and karate black belt. "Training and skill are much more important than muscle fibers. Karate is skill and not a mere performance of muscle activity. We think people are quick when they don't telegraph a technique and slow when they do. People tell me, for instance, that I have a quick backfist. Now, I know I'm not that fast—I just have the ability to throw it without telegraphing it."

In addition to muscles and tendons, you have ligaments which are fibrous bands that hold the bones together at the joints. Muscles and tendons have elasticity, but ligaments do not. When stretched, ligaments remain in a lengthened state. When this occurs, the joint lacks stability and may be susceptible to chronic dislocation. This is particularly true of weight-bearing joints such as the knee.

"Ligaments don't have elasticity; once they are stretched, they are stretched," Bryan Robbins told me. "Tendons do come back but once you stretch the ligaments in your shoulders, for example, what they have to do is fold it over and staple it."

When doing flexibility exercises, are you stretching muscles, tendons or ligaments, I asked Robbins.

"Hopefully not the ligaments," he answers. "Because if you get them to the point where they're ripped, they won't come back without surgery. Basically, you are stretching the tendons and muscles."

A pulled muscle is a tear of muscle fibers and is indicated by a sharp and persistent pain. Don't continue to exercise at this point, as you will further injure the muscle. There is no treatment to make the muscle heal any faster. The immediate treatment has been referred to as ICE: ice, compression, and elevation. Ice and compression (bandages) should be discontinued after twenty-four hours. Elevation should continue as long as there is swelling. Many physicians recommend the use of heat after forty-eight hours to increase the blood supply to the injured muscle.

Muscle soreness usually settles in eight to twenty-four hours after exercise. If the pain is sharp and localized, it may mean an injury such as a tear. Most muscle soreness, however, is due to a swelling of the muscle fibers which have been stretched by repeated contractions or to a build-up of lactic acid. Lactic acid is an exercise breakdown product that accumulates in the muscles after a particularly strenuous

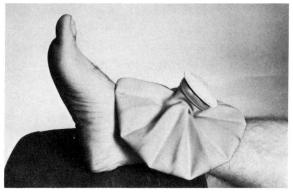

Fig. 28 The treatment recommended by doctors for most soft-tissue and muscle/bone injuries can be abbreviated ICE. Ice decreases the blood flow to the injured area. The more blood collects there, the longer it takes to heal. (Heat, incidentally, will cause increased swelling and make the injury worse if applied at first. Only add heat after seventy-two hours.) Compression limits swelling, which can prolong healing. Elevation helps to drain excess fluid which collects in an injured area.

Some doctors add a fourth letter to the formula, *R,* which stands for rest of an injured part until it heals to a proper stage.

workout. A cooling-down period after the hardest part of the workout helps to counter its buildup.

What about cartilage injuries?

"I've had three cartilages taken out of my knees, which weren't karate related, incidentally, and it hasn't slowed me down as far as karate is concerned," says Paul Hinkley. "Once cartilage is torn, there is very little healing because it is not living tissue with an adequate blood supply, and so whatever you do with it, as far as rehabilitation is concerned, is just preventing further damage. There is a lot of prevention one can do after a cartilage tear, providing it is not a significant tear that requires surgery. Surgery recovery is fairly quick, however, and you can be back out kicking within a few weeks."

Hinkley teachers both karate and yoga at Richland College and at SMU in Dallas. Because he has had several knee injuries, I asked him about things to do to prevent them.

"I think it's important to have tension in the leg and foot and probably even keep the leg slightly bent all the time when the kick is thrown so there is no hyperextension of the knee. You can do that in the same way you throw a punch without straightening the arm out. I think if you kick with good tension in the foot, like pulling the toes back, your leg never really straightens."

Some instructors advocate doing the majority of your leg training on a bag. Not only is there some resistance so that the leg doesn't hyperextend, but it is good training for power and focus in your kick.

"Kicking in mid-air is not particularly good for your knees," says former karate champion Jim Butin. "All the shock of that kick is going to the weakest part of the leg, and that's the knee. Over a period of time those ligaments are going to stretch, especially if you lock the leg out. Why not have even a light target to hit to take some of that force off the knee? We use kicking shields in our school. Training aids are also more realistic, as it gives someone an idea of how strong his kicks really are."

"Rehabilitation exercise after a knee injury includes leg extensions and leg curls," says Hinkley. "Even leg presses or squats without straightening the knee are all valuable. You want to build up the muscle around the joint."

Muscles contract but tendons don't. A tendon rupture occurs when a tendon separates from a bone. The pain is severe and sometimes you can hear a pop. If you suspect this injury apply the ICE treatment and call the doctor.

All right, let's talk about the actual stretching routine itself. Before you start, remember to warm up. Warming up increases the blood supply to the muscles and raises their temperature slightly, making them more pliable and less prone to injury.

According to physiologists, there are basically two types

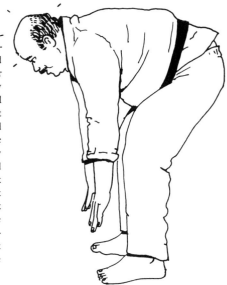

Fig. 38 Even if you were a professional athlete your body would lose its conditioning in a matter of a few short weeks without any exercise. Sports physiologists call this process "reversibility." Most martial artists who have stopped training for a few months have experienced this fact after they come back to the dojo and find that they are amazingly short of breath during the workout because the muscles have lost some of their ability to utilize oxygen efficiently, and are extremely sore after the workout because the muscle fibers are more susceptible to tearing.

of stretching, *passive* and *active*. Passive, or static, stretching involves a slow sustained stretching of a muscle. You slowly lengthen the muscle and hold it in the lengthened position for several seconds. When martial artists spread their legs and grasp an ankle with each hand and hold their head to the floor, it is an example of passive stretching.

Active, or ballistic, stretching involves bouncing or jerking to gain momentum in a body part to increase the amount of stretch that can be placed on the muscle. Swinging the leg up to the front or side is an example of active stretching. So is spreading the legs out in a sitting position and bouncing the head down to the floor. Because you are forcefully moving the joints to the extreme in this kind of exercise, you increase the potential of the "stretch reflex." This means that the very muscle being stretched will instead contract. Obviously, the active stretch should be done with great care.

"I recommend that you stretch statically first and then do some kind of bounce stretch," says Robbins. "By static stretch, I mean holding a position for anywhere from five to thirty seconds. Some people say if it doesn't hurt it isn't good, but I don't advocate that at all because I think pain is your body telling you you've gone too far. There's a difference between a stretched feeling and pain. If it really hurts then just back off a little bit and try to relax.

"Also I've found that concentrating on breathing can help your stretching," continues Robbins. "We are born with potential in each of our body parts. You may be real tight in the hips and may never be able to get head-high side kicks, but you still work on it.

"What you don't use, you lose," he warns. "If you don't continue to work on your flexibility, you lose it. Now once gained, you don't need to work as hard to keep it. I recommend stretching a minimum of three days a week, and you could even stretch every day. If you are trying to achieve muscular gains, like trying to make your arms stronger, you should only work those muscles three days a week. But you could stretch every single day with no detrimental effects to the body."

Although partner stretching is often used by athletic trainers and physical therapists, through years of experience, they have developed a feel for the right stretching force. It should be done very carefully by the untrained person.

Paul Hinkley told me, "One study indicated that in karate the fewest injuries were in kata practice, the next smallest number was in prearranged choreographed sparring, and the next in free-sparring, but the greatest number of karate injuries took place in partner stretching. That indicates that by working with an untrained partner, people were putting so much pressure on the muscles that it was completely unnatural and they were injuring themselves. That was the highest incidence of karate injuries, at least in that one study.

"I've seen instructors that had the students sit cross-legged with their backs to the wall while another student stood on their knees. That's pretty foolish," says Hinkley. "The instructor should either decrease partner stretching or do it with a great deal of care to avoid people stressing other people. Have it completely controlled by the individual being stretched so they control the activity."

WEIGHT TRAINING
for the Martial Arts

You've probably heard it said that weight lifting makes you stronger but slower. But Rob Allemier, a long-time weight lifter and martial artist, has other ideas. "Anyone who states that probably went into a free-weight gym and saw all those hulks and said, 'My God, look at how big those guys are, and how slow they are.' But most weight lifters have not been trained in any other kind of skills," he advises.

Allemier is executive vice-president of the American Taekwon-Do Association and runs fitness centers and martial arts schools in Michigan and Texas. "Look at professional football players. They are monsters and very well built, but you can't tell me they are slow. They are very quick. The difference is reflex timing. If a guy is real big and strong but can't touch his toes because he is so muscle-bound, (it's because) he hasn't been taught any skills except taking the collars off the ends of the weights," says Allemier.

Allemier believes in weight training not as an end in itself but as a training tool for the martial artist. Allemier has run through the whole weight spectrum from free weights to a universal set-up and finally to the nautilus machines. "It's a proven fact that the better your musculature, the better athlete you will be," he says. "With free weights I always seemed to injure myself, and I had to have a partner to train with. Also, I didn't really want to go to the gym and spend two or more hours to get in a workout.

"I liked the universal system because I could get through my workout quicker, but I didn't seem to get the same results or the same 'burn' as I did with the free weights," he says. "Nautilus is the best weight-training equipment on the market. You can do a really good workout in 30 or 45 minutes."

Fig. 29 This machine works the quadriceps (the large thigh muscle) which is used for all martial arts kicks.

Fig. 30–31 The lateral raise works the shoulders for jabs.

Allemier points out that nautilus equipment is broken down to isolate every muscle group. Here he demonstrates six different exercises perfect for the martial artist. But Allemier also realizes not everyone can afford to sign up at a fancy fitness center and recommends setting up a gym in your own home. "Get a pipe and mount it in your basement where you can do chin-ups and where you can hang your legs over it and do upside down sit-ups. Maybe you can build yourself a Roman chair out of two-by-fours to do your sit-ups. With all that plus some push-ups, you could have a helluva workout," he says. "The only thing you really can't get to is your legs, but if you buy a cheap set of weights, say 110 pounds, you can do some squats."

Some students working out on their own like to use ankle weights to improve their kicks. "If a person is of advanced rank and knows how to use them slowly, then there is nothing wrong with it. But what happens with the younger students is they kick and punch as hard and as fast as they can," says Allemier. "That pops the joints apart, stretches the ligaments and tendons, and makes the whole joint weak. For that reason, I am totally against ankle weights for the beginner."

Fig. 32-33 The overhead press works the shoulders and the triceps which are used for reverse punches.

Fig. 34-37 The biceps/triceps exercise is good
for strength in the shoulders, arms, and wrists.
All martial artists need this.

Nutrition

By itself, a good diet won't guarantee you better performance in your martial arts practice. Some champions are vegetarians; some believe in fasting; others eat blood-red meat; and others are junk-food junkies. There are too many variables to be able to point to just one thing and say, "This is the secret." Still, most people agree that a balanced diet is important to anyone involved in strenuous physical activity like the martial arts.

While some people never think about their diet, others spend hundreds of dollars monthly on "health foods," vitamin supplements, mineral supplements, and drugs. How necessary is this? It is the opinion of most nutritionists that everything the body needs can be supplied by a properly balanced diet. About the only additional things an athlete needs are more calories and more fluids. A balanced diet will give you the nutrients that are found in the six components of food: water, carbohydrate, fat, protein, vitamins, and minerals.

Protein is the primary structural material of cells and tissues. It is not a source of immediate energy, and protein requirements do not increase with exercise. The body cannot store excess protein. Protein contains twenty-three different amino acids, but the body can manufacture only fourteen of them. Therefore, we must get the other nine so-called essential amino acids from what we eat. There are two kinds of protein food sources: complete, containing all nine essential amino acids, and incomplete, containing less than nine. Meat is usually a complete protein source, but vegetarians can get their nine essential amino acids by combining corn, for instance, which has seven, and beans, which have the missing two.

I asked Joyce Oldenburg, a nutritionist, about the difference between proteins and carbohydrate.

"They are different in their chemical structure," she told me. "Carbohydrates are composed of carbons, hydrogens, and oxygens (that's where the name comes from). Proteins have nitrogen, whereas the carbohydrates do not. Carbohydrates are more easily digested by the body. They are used mostly for energy purposes, while proteins are used as building blocks."

Because muscle is composed of protein, some trainers believe that protein supplements make muscles bigger or stronger. However, the only time that protein supplements are necessary is when the athlete is not eating protein in his regular diet, which is almost never the case with the average American. Studies have shown that a protein-rich diet does not improve performance or make one stronger.

"Once you get more than the body can use, protein is used as energy or stored as fat; and, it is an expensive form of energy or fat," says Oldenburg.

So, are carbohydrates better, I wanted to know?

"Carbohydrate, fat, and protein are all needed if the body is to function normally—one is not 'better' than the other. Carbohydrate is a more efficient, less expensive source of energy. Each person, depending on a number of factors (age, sex, and so on) can be directed by the table of Recommended Dietary Allowances. Now, an athlete that is under more physical stress will have greater allowances than the normal person, but once you go past what your body really needs, the extra protein doesn't do that much good."

I asked Joyce about the carbohydrate packing theory, which was devised in Sweden in the 1960s.

"There are several different views on that," she answered. "Basically, it involves eating very little carbohydrate five or six days before a competition (this is called the depletion stage) but eating a lot of it the last two or three days. The theory is that your body is more able to efficiently use the new supply of carbohydrate and that it provides more energy for a longer period of time than is normal."

There is some debate as to whether the depletion stage is necessary, and it could even be dangerous. Some have linked it to cramps and kidney congestion. Even so, many endurance athletes, like long distance runners and swimmers, swear by it.

This brings up the question of what kinds of food contain carbohydrate and what foods contain protein.

"Carbohydrate generally comes from plants, vegetables, potatoes, whole grains, fruits, things like that," says Oldenburg. "Proteins are usually from animal sources like milk, cheese, and meats."

Don't eat just before a tournament or even before a class because, in order to facilitate digestion, the stomach requires a larger supply of blood than normal. When you exercise hard, however, the heart pumps more blood to the other muscles and the stomach muscles start to cramp from lack of oxygen. How long your stomach takes to digest your food depends on a number of factors. If you are in better shape you can reduce the time between eating and working out. If the exercise you will be doing will be in a stressful situation, like a belt exam or tournament, you will need to allow a little longer for the stomach to empty because the stress slows down the digestion process. Generally speaking, the pre-workout meal should be high in carbohydrates, low in protein, and contain plenty of liquid. Lots of athletes eat pancakes, fruits, bread, or spaghetti before a competition because they are high in carbohydrate.

"If your competition is in the morning," warns Oldenburg, "you just want to have a light breakfast of fruit or cereal and milk rather than something with a lot of fat in it, like sausages or hash-browns, because that's going to take a longer time for the body to digest. You want something that the body can get into the system quickly."

Incidentally, lots of people think that sugar, because it is pure carbohydrate, is a good pre-competition meal. But while a candy bar is a quick source of energy, a sugar-loaded meal (honey, syrup, soft drinks, and so on) can cause a *low*-sugar level to occur in the blood two to five hours later because the body releases so much insulin to bring the high level of sugar back down. Low blood sugar can cause tiredness and stomach cramps.

The average American eats too much red meat, salt, and sugar. Many nutritionists recommend the restriction of these foodstuffs. You should probably eat more fruits, vegetables, whole grains, poultry, fish, and skim milk instead.

"Other than perhaps a little more protein, I don't think an athlete's nutritional requirements are much different than that for a noncompetitive person," says Oldenburg. "I think most people, athletes or not, should probably take some kind of vitamin and mineral supplement because a lot of the foods we eat today are refined or are convenience foods—a lot of the vitamins and minerals have been cooked or frozen out of them."

You might be interested in knowing what vitamins are. They are components of enzymes that regulate the rate of bodily chemical processes. They are not a direct source of energy and you don't need more of them just because you exercise a lot. Using vitamins in place of a meal, incidentally, makes no sense at all.

"The only way we knew we needed vitamins is by analyzing the diets of those people with vitamin deficiency diseases [such as rickets, scurvy, and so on]," says Oldenburg. "Most of what we know about vitamins is still based on deficiencies and how to prevent them. There is a whole new area, which as yet nutritionists know very little about, which involves using vitamins as drugs—the emphasis being not on just maintaining good health, but using drugs to enhance performance and cure nondeficiency diseases (like cancer).

"As I said, I think most people should take some kind of supplement, maybe a one-a-day type, but not megadoses of vitamins. A megadose is a thousand times what the normal requirement is. There are many problems that arise if you get too much of even a good thing like vitamins [kidney stones, rebound scurvy, and so on]," Oldenburg says.

According to most nutritionists and doctors, large doses of vitamin supplements don't beef up performance, don't improve strength or endurance, and don't prevent injuries or colds. Overdoses have been proved to be dangerous. Massive doses of vitamin C, for example, which many people down in amounts fifty times their daily requirement, have been linked to diarrhea, decreased fertility, and kidney stones. Overdoses of vitamin E, which some claim boosts sexual potency, have proved toxic to laboratory rats. Suffice it to say that if you eat a balanced diet and take a one-a-day supplement, you will never need or want to take megadoses of vitamins.

Minerals are basic elements found in the soil. They are absorbed by plants and then by animals that eat the plants. Your body needs minerals to form chemicals that regulate the bodily processes. One of the minerals your body needs is sodium (salt), but it has been well established that the average American's daily diet contains so much salt that you should think about cutting down rather than taking salt tablets (even when working out heavily). Other minerals that athletes do need are magnesium and potassium. These can usually be well supplied by just eating a balanced diet, but you might want to take a daily vitamin with minerals added.

"Food and nutrition are very important," concludes kung fu champion Eric Lee. "When the body is clean the mind feels good. That is the yin/yang balance. I wish I had known more about how to have balanced energy when I was competing. Sometimes I would overtrain, and that's when you need more rest and more supplement to your diet," he says.

Psyching Out Your Opponent

Ray McCallum has been rated in the top five fighters in the country for the last five years. He's been competing since he was a young teenager and has grown accustomed to the pressure found in a karate ring. But in 1979 he traveled to Japan and learned a real lesson in mental pressure. He had gone there to fight a full-contact bout with the Japanese kick-boxing champion.

"Although the man was actually kind of slow and predictable—he was a monster," Raymond told me. "I side kicked him into the ropes and his expression never changed. He was totally conditioned, physically and mentally, to take anything I had. I hit him with everything, jabs, kicks— it didn't have any effect on him—but it began to have a psychological effect on me. I said to myself, "What am I supposed to do to this guy?" I was ahead on points for the first four rounds, but when the bell rang at the end of the fourth round he dropped me with a kick as I turned to go to my corner.

"When I came out for the fifth round," says McCallum, "I was still dazed, and that's when he started kicking my legs (something that is illegal in American competition). I was too tired to skip back like before and he was kicking hard, knocking me down. My legs started to cramp up and I was scared. Finally, after about the fifth time I had gone down, I said, 'Throw in the towel. I want to go home.'"

McCallum had learned his lessons about how to psych out an opponent. Today he uses the same techniques, training both his mind and body to withstand punishment.

"When I take a good shot," says McCallum, "I try to just smile at the guy. That can really shake them up."

"You need to learn how to conquer other people's minds," agrees Tommy Williams, a rising full-contact fighter from Oklahoma City. "Always attack the opponent's mind.

The center of action is there. If you can tear down their mind, their defenses must come down as well.

"Every martial artist should understand the nature of his own mind and instincts," continues Williams. "Everything is based on that instinct. A good fighter is like a psychologist. He is aware of the fact that if he does a certain thing it causes certain reactions from his opponent."

Aikido instructor Bill Sosa gave me a good example of this when he told me this story.

"I had this guy come into my shop (Sosa runs a martial arts supply store in Dallas) and says he is a student of a jujutsu instructor I know. Well, this guy is about 220 and his arm's as big as my thigh. He says that his instructor has a hard time bending his wrist and he heard I have good ki and so he wants to know if I can bend his wrist.

"Well, I hate that kind of stuff but I say okay and he sticks out this arm that looks like a leg," says Sosa. "Now, if I had just tried to bend his wrist with muscle power I couldn't have done it, but by giving him a little jerk [and he jerks my wrist down to illustrate] I can get his *mind* off his wrist and then bend it, like so [and he does a kotegashi throw on me]."

"Mental attitude is just as important as physical skill even in kata competition," says Eric Lee, famed forms champion. "Everybody has stage fright where you are afraid of the other competitors. Some try to psych themselves up to feel more power. Ignore them," advises Lee. "Don't start thinking, 'This guy is good,' or you've already given him a point.

"Before it's your turn to compete, go talk to someone, your instructor, if possible, to give you moral support. If I see my student, I look in his eye and I tell him, 'You look good. I think you can do it.' If there is no one there [to talk to], do isometric exercises, stretch, something.

"In a tournament everyone tries to psych each other out," says Lee. "I remember one guy trying to do that in a big kata competition. He'd ask me how long I had trained and so on. I had one guy come up to me and use bad language and everything. He has a girlfriend there that kept looking at me although I had no interest in her. So I went up to him and I said, 'Is that your girlfriend? Well, she keeps looking at me. I don't know why, but I just wanted you to know.' He got so mad he forgot his form. If someone tries to psych you out, then do it to them.

"You have to have an ego to win," says Lee. "Some have bad egos—some good. If you want something bad enough you can have it. There's nothing wrong with that," he says. "But remember that it is not bad to lose either. You can learn from it. Be optimistic. You lose—big deal—you will do better next time."

Lee believes that meditation is one good way to work on your mental discipline and attitude. He advises rest and meditation after a hard workout.

"I think kata training is another good way to help your mental attitude," says current number one forms champion George Chung. "In kata you are working on your concentration, you are working on disciplining yourself because you are working alone. Kata helps you prepare to train by yourself. After all, when you are competing you are by yourself."

When you work on your kata try to imagine an opponent in front of you at every step. Block his strike as hard as you can and penetrate with your own blows. Know why you are doing something and it will seem much more practical to you. Well-done forms train you mentally and physically, and they are even fun if you approach them with the right spirit.

CHAPTER EIGHT

A Martial Arts Dictionary

Aikido. Morohei Ueshiba's system that he developed from more ancient Japanese arts. Noted for its strictly defensive attitudes and extensive use of the concept of ki force, aikido relies almost exclusively on throws and takedowns.

Arnis. A Filipino art that utilizes both empty-handed and weapons techniques such as the stick and knife. Also known as kali (the ancient name) and escrima.

Atemi. Japanese. The art of striking vital areas.

Bando. A Burmese martial art utilizing both empty-handed and weapons techniques.

Bersilat. A Malaysian martial art which uses weapons as well as empty-hand strikes and throws.

Black belt. Rank denoting expert in Japanese, Okinawan, and Korean martial arts. Traditionally there was no rank in the Chinese arts; however, many American kung fu instructors have adopted a similar system with either a black belt or black sash. In most systems there are ten degrees of black belt, with the tenth degree reserved for the one recognized master of the style.

Bodhidharma. The Indian Buddhist monk who traveled to the Shaolin Monastary in China in A.D. 525 and started his system of spiritual and physical discipline, which many claim to be the parent system for all of the martial arts. (See illustration on page 7.)

Bokken. Japanese wooden sword used for practice.

Budo. Japanese term meaning martial ways which sprang up in the late 18th century. The do arts are designed to function as a philosophy of life encompassing more than just physical techniques of fighting.

Bujutsu. Japanese term meaning martial arts. The forerunner to budo. The jutsu arts were, by and large, more concerned with the warring applications of the fighting arts.

Bushi. Literally "martial man." Another term for the samurai, the feudal Japanese warriors.

Bushido. The code of ethics of the bushi. Similar to the European medieval knight's code of chivalry.

Ch'i. The Chinese concept of the flowing energy of life. It traces its philosophical roots back to Taoism and Buddhism. The internal arts spend much time on learning to control ch'i flow and apply it to both destructive and healing applications (i.e., acupuncture).

Ch'uan fa. The ancient name of the fighting system of the Shaolin Monks.

Dan. Degree ranking within black belt.

Dim mak. The Chinese death touch. Kung fu masters were supposedly able to cause a delayed and fatal sickness after only touching a vital spot on a person's body.

Do. Path or way. Japanese description of a complete philosophical system of martial practice.

Dojo. Traditionally, the training hall where the Japanese arts are taught and practiced. (Dojang in Korean.)

Five animals. The movements of the dragon, tiger, leopard, crane, and snake form the basis for many kung fu techniques. (See illustration on page 89.)

Form. Choreographed training patterns used for practice of balance, stances, technical perfection of power and breath control. Called "sets" in Chinese systems and frequently called "kata," which is Japanese. Most karate tournaments have kata competitions as well as fighting divisions.

Full-contact karate. Professional sport where the winner is determined by points or knockout as in boxing. Contestants must wear pads on their hands and feet. Many traditional karate instructors frown on this modification of their art, while others welcome the exposure that it has generated. There are three sanctioning bodies for full contact in America, the PKA (Professional Karate Association), the WKA (World Karate Association), and KICK (Karate International Council for Kick-boxing). Each has its own rules.

Gi. The uniform worn by martial arts practitioners. The judogi differs from the karategi in that it must be much heavier and double layered because of the grappling nature of the art. (Tobak is the Korean term, but almost everyone uses the Japanese nomenclature in America.)

Gung fu. See kung fu.

Hajime. Japanese for "begin." Used in judo and karate tournaments to start a match.

Hakama. The long divided skirt worn over the gi-pants in several Japanese arts, for example aikido.

Hapkido. A Korean style of fighting founded by Yong Shul Choi around 1940 by combining Japanese aiki-jutsu and native Korean systems like hwarang-do and tae kyon (later tae kwon-do).

Hwarang-do. The code followed by the hwarang warriors of ancient Korea. It is also today a fighting art and healing system.

Iaido. The art of drawing the Japanese sword practiced by the samurai as iaijutsu.

Jeet kune do. Bruce Lee's system, born in 1967 out of his desire to free his students from the mold of any particular style. Literally it means "way of the intercepting fist."

Judo. Jigoro Kano's innovative sport and self-defense, which he founded in 1882. Primarily a grappling and throwing art, it is by far the largest standardized martial art. No matter where in the world you train, the terminology and techniques remain the same.

Ju-jutsu. Known as the "flexible art" or the "gentle art," this ancient Japanese system of combat includes a huge variety of empty-handed techniques as well as some weapons usage.

Kalari payat. An ancient form of South Indian martial art.

Karate. Literally "empty hand." Also known as karate do, it is probably the most widely recognized martial art in the United States. Originally from Okinawa, it is a striking rather than a grappling art. It has become a generic term referring to not only Okinawan and Japanese systems but Korean and the newer American eclectic styles as well.

Kata. See form.

Kendo. A popular (in Japan) modern derivation of the ancient samurai art of sword play, ken-jutsu. For competition the kendoka (practitioner) wears leather armor and uses a bamboo sword.

Ki. Literally "spirit" in Japanese. Corresponds to the Chinese ch'i. Control of this vital force is frequently practiced in arts like ju-jutsu and aikido where it is important to control an opponent's ki to throw or hold him. It is seen in karate training as well, where the emphasis is more often on using ki force to break through an opponent's defenses with a strike.

Kiai. The yell, literally "spirit shout," used in Japanese and other martial arts usually just before or just at the moment of contact. (Kiap in Korean).

Kobudo. An Okinawan system of weapons usage. The most frequently seen weapons include the *bo* (six foot staff), the *sai* (a three-pronged short sword), the *kama* (sickle), the *tonfa* (originally a wooden grain grinder), and the *nunchaku* (the two pieces of wood connected by a rope or chain that Bruce Lee made famous in his movies).

Kodokan. The name Jigoro Kano gave to his art of judo. Today it is the center of judo training and administration in Tokyo. Literally "the hall for teaching the way."

Kshatriya. The warrior caste of old India. Some speculate that Bodhidharma was a member of this caste while a young man in India and learned his fighting skills in that way.

Kukkiwon. The huge headquarters for the World Tae Kwon-Do Federation in Seoul.

Kuk sool won. A Korean art similar to ju-jutsu in that it utilizes kicks and punches as well as joint-locking techniques.

Kung fu. Literally means "high quality" or "skilled." Has come to refer to the many Chinese systems of fighting. The Cantonese pronunciation is gung fu.

Kyu. Grade or rank below black belt in Japanese martial arts. (Gup in Korean.)

Kyudo. The modern Japanese sport of archery derived from the ancient combat archery of feudal Japan, Kyu-jutsu.

Mu shin. The Zen concept of "no mind." Used by the samurai to overcome the fear of death.

Ninjutsu. Sometimes called the "art of invisibility," it was the feudal Japanese discipline of espionage and assassination. During Japan's warring period from the thirteenth to the seventeenth century, the art was passed down from father to son. There were few outsiders in a ninja clan. A ninja always concealed his identity, never appearing in public without a disguise. Cultural opposites of the samurai, the ninja made extensive use of unique weapons such as darts and throwing stars as well as the more traditional empty-handed and weapons techniques. He was an expert escape artist, being able to manipulate his joints to slip out of knots. Ninjutsu was banned with the unification of Japan in the seventeenth century, but a handful of men continued to practice in secret.

Pentjak silat. An ancient Indonesian martial art making use of both weaponless and weapons techniques.

Randori. Free style practice in judo and aikido where students can practice their techniques.

Ryu. Japanese for "school" or "tradition." (Kwan is Korean for "school.")

Sambo. A Russian form of wrestling where the contestants wear jackets, kind of like a cross between Western wrestling and Japanese judo.

Samurai. See bushi.

Sanchin. Breathing exercise in Okinawan karate where the body is tensed to improve breath and muscle power. (See illustration on page 55.)

Savate. The French system of kick-fighting which has grown to include hand techniques and high kicks since its formal organization in 1824 by Michael Casseuse, who had studied the old kick-fighting styles of the Paris street brawlers.

Sensei. Japanese for "teacher" or "experienced one." Most often used to refer to a martial arts teacher, but is also used in Japan for other respected masters such as artisans.

Shaolin temple. The Chinese Buddhist monastery where Bodhidharma is said to have first organized martial practice.

Shiatsu. A Japanese massage technique used to relieve pain from injuries and to improve flexibility. (See illustration on page 119.)

Shihan. Japanese for master instructor.

Shuriken. Small pointed iron throwing weapons including darts, spikes, and the often seen star. See also *Ninjutsu.* (See illustration on page 93.)

Sifu. Cantonese for "master." Used for kung fu teachers.

Soke. Japanese for head of a style or founder of the system.

Sumo. A traditional form of Japanese wrestling quite popular in that country. Two men, usually huge, try to either push one another outside of the ring or force the opponent to touch the mat above the knee.

Tae kwon-do. The name (way of kicking and punching) was coined in 1955 by Choi Hong Hi to refer to the ancient Korean fighting arts, previously known as taekyon and subak among others. Noted for its high and powerful kicks, it is mainly a weaponless, hard-style fighting system.

Tai chi chuan. A soft internal art popular in China and elsewhere, primarily as a means of promoting health and longevity. It is largely based on the Taoist concept of ch'i.

Tao. Chinese term meaning "path" or "way." A philosophical system going back to the fourth century writings of Lao Tzu.

Te. Literally "hand." The Okinawan style formulated from Chinese ch'uan fa and the old Okinawa-te, which eventually was taken to Japan by Gichin Funakoshi in 1922 and became karate.

Thai kick boxing. Also called muay thai, it is a popular (in

Thailand and Japan) but brutal sport where almost anything except throws or biting is allowed.

Tien hsueh. Chinese art of striking vital areas. Analogous to atemi in Japanese.

Ukemi. The art of falling used in judo and aikido.

Wushu. The official name for the martial arts in mainland China. It is practiced mainly for exercise and sport, as the government has frowned on any philosophical trappings.

Yang. The positive side of the universe in Taoist philosophy. Fullness, sun, hardness, male. (See illustration on page 101.)

Yin. The opposite of Yang. Negative side, or emptiness, darkness, softness, female.

Zen. An offshoot of Buddhism which believes that through intense meditation one can achieve enlightenment.

Index

185